LIGHT THROUGH DARKNESS

TRADITIONS OF CHRISTIAN SPIRITUALITY SERIES

At the Fountain of Elijah: The Carmelite Tradition
Wilfrid McGreal, o. carm.

Brides in the Desert: The Spirituality of the Beguines
Saskia Murk-Jansen

Contemplation and Compassion: The Victorine Tradition
Steven Chase

Eyes to See, Ears to Hear: An Introduction to Ignatian Spirituality
David Lonsdale

Following in the Footsteps of Christ: The Anabaptist Tradition
C. Arnold Snyder

God's Lovers in an Age of Anxiety: The Medieval English Mystics
Joan M. Nuth

Heart Speaks to Heart: The Salesian Tradition
Wendy M. Wright

Journeys on the Edges: The Celtic Tradition
Thomas O'Loughlin

The Language of Silence: The Changing Face of Monastic Solitude
Peter-Damian Belisle, OSB Cam

Mysticism and Prophecy: The Dominican Tradition
Richard Woods, OP

Our Restless Heart: The Augustinian Tradition
Thomas F. Martin, OSA

The Poetic Imagination: An Anglican Spiritual Tradition
L. William Countryman

Poverty and Joy: The Franciscan Tradition
William J. Short, OFM

Prayer and Community: The Benedictine Tradition
Columba Stewart, OSB

Silence and Witness: The Quaker Tradition
Michael L. Birkel

Standing in God's Holy Fire: The Byzantine Spiritual Tradition
John Anthony McGuckin

The Spirit of Worship: The Liturgical Tradition
Susan J. White

The Way of Simplicity: The Cistercian Tradition
Esther de Waal

LIGHT THROUGH DARKNESS

The Orthodox Tradition

JOHN CHRYSSAVGIS

SERIES EDITOR:
Philip Sheldrake

ORBIS BOOKS
Maryknoll, New York 10545

Founded in 1970, Orbis Books endeavors to publish works that enlighten the mind, nourish the spirit, and challenge the conscience. The publishing arm of the Maryknoll Fathers & Brothers, Orbis seeks to explore the global dimensions of the Christian faith and mission, to invite dialogue with diverse cultures and religious traditions, and to serve the cause of reconciliation and peace. The books published reflect the views of their authors and do not represent the official position of the Society. To learn more about Maryknoll and Orbis Books, please visit our website at www.maryknoll.org.

First published in Great Britian in 2004 by
Darton, Longman and Todd Ltd
1 Spencer Court
140-142 Wandsworth High Street
London SW18 4JJ

First published in the USA in 2004 by
Orbis Books
P.O. Box 308
Maryknoll, New York 10545-0308
U.S.A.

Copyright © 2004 by John Chryssavgis

Orbis ISBN 1–57075–548–5

Printed and bound in Great Britain.

Library of Congress Cataloguing-in-Publication Data

Chryssavgis, John.
    Light through darkness : the Orthodox tradition / John Chryssavgis.
        p. cm. – (Traditions of Christian spirituality)
    Includes bibliographical references.
    ISBN 1–57075–548–5 (pbk.)
    1. Spirituality—Orthodox Eastern Chruch.   I. Title.   II. Series.
        BX382.C493   2004
        281.9—dc22

                                                              2004010798

CONTENTS

duende

a gypsy word, meaning 'spirit of the earth'
(F. Garcia Lorca)

the cry of the heart
the spirit rising from the depths,
mixing with the earth in equal measure our tears and blood

(Jamie Moran, Poorwolf)

ACKNOWLEDGEMENTS

The grace of God has taught me – or, at least, provided me with ample opportunities through others to learn – that the true light only comes from within the darkness, when the latter is embraced until everything inside us and around us is transformed into light. Without these opportunities, I would not be who I am.

I am grateful to Clinton Minnaar of Cape Town in South Africa for his generous time and gracious counsel.

Earlier versions of sections in this book appeared in *Theology Today* 58, 3; *Cistercian Studies Quarterly* 34, 4 and 37, 4; *Paths to the Heart* (WorldWisdom/Fons Vitae, 2002); and *Presence: Journal of Spiritual Directors International* 8, 3.

PREFACE TO THE SERIES

Nowadays, in the Western world, there is a widespread hunger
for spirituality in all its forms. This is not confined to traditional religious people, let alone to regular churchgoers. The
desire for resources to sustain the spiritual quest has led many
people to seek wisdom in unfamiliar places. Some have turned
to cultures other than their own. The fascination with Native
American or Aboriginal Australian spiritualities is a case in
point. Other people have been attracted by the religions of
India and Tibet or the Jewish Kabbalah and Sufi mysticism.
One problem is that, in comparison to other religions, Christianity is not always associated in people's minds with 'spirituality'. The exceptions are a few figures from the past who have
achieved almost cult status such as Hildegard of Bingen or
Meister Eckhart. This is a great pity, for Christianity East and
West over two thousand years has given birth to an immense
range of spiritual wisdom. Many traditions continue to be
active today. Others that were forgotten are being rediscovered
and reinterpreted.

It is a long time since an extended series of introductions to
Christian spiritual traditions has been available in English.
Given the present climate, it is an opportune moment for a new
series which will help more people to be aware of the great
spiritual riches available within the Christian traditions.

The overall purpose of the series is to make selected spiritual
traditions available to a contemporary readership. The books
seek to provide accurate and balanced historical and thematic
treatments of their subjects. The authors are also conscious of
the need to make connections with contemporary experience

and values without being artificial or reducing a tradition to one dimension. The authors are well versed in reliable scholarship about the traditions they describe. However, their intention is that the books should be fresh in style and accessible to the general reader.

One problem that such a series inevitably faces is the word 'spirituality'. For example, it is increasingly used beyond religious circles and does not necessarily imply a faith tradition. Again, it could mean substantially different things for a Christian and a Buddhist. Within Christianity itself, the word in its modern sense is relatively recent. The reality that it stands for differs subtly in the different contexts of time and place. Historically, 'spirituality' covers a breadth of human experience and a wide range of values and practices.

No single definition of 'spirituality' has been imposed on the authors in this series. Yet, despite the breadth of the series there is a sense of a common core in the writers themselves and in the traditions they describe. All Christian spiritual traditions have their source in three things. First, while drawing on ordinary experience and even religious insights from elsewhere, Christian spiritualities are rooted in the Scriptures and particularly in the Gospels. Second, spiritual traditions are not derived from abstract theory but from attempts to live out gospel values in a positive yet critical way within specific historical and cultural contexts. Third, the experiences and insights of individuals and groups are not isolated but are related to the wider Christian tradition of beliefs, practices and community life. From a Christian perspective, spirituality is not just concerned with prayer or even with narrowly religious activities. It concerns the whole of human life, viewed in terms of a conscious relationship with God, in Jesus Christ, through the indwelling of the Holy Spirit and within a community of believers.

The series as a whole includes traditions that probably would not have appeared twenty years ago. The authors themselves have been encouraged to challenge, where appropriate, inaccurate assumptions about their particular tradition. While conscious of their own biases, authors have none the less sought to correct the imbalances of the past. Previous understandings of what is mainstream or 'orthodox' sometimes need to be questioned. People or practices that became marginal demand to be re-examined. Studies of spirituality in the past frequently underestimated or ignored the role of women. Sometimes the treatments of spiritual traditions were culturally one-sided because they were written from an uncritical Western European or North Atlantic perspective.

However, any series is necessarily selective. It cannot hope to do full justice to the extraordinary variety of Christian spiritual traditions. The principles of selection are inevitably open to question. I hope that an appropriate balance has been maintained between a sense of the likely readership on the one hand and the dangers of narrowness on the other. In the end, choices had to be made and the result is inevitably weighted in favour of traditions that have achieved 'classic' status or which seem to capture the contemporary imagination. Within these limits, I trust that the series will offer a reasonably balanced account of what the Christian spiritual tradition has to offer.

As editor of the series I would like to thank all the authors who agreed to contribute and for the stimulating conversations and correspondence that sometimes resulted. I am especially grateful for the high quality of their work which made my task so much easier. Editing such a series is a complex undertaking. I have worked closely throughout with the editorial team of Darton, Longman and Todd and Robert Ellsberg of Orbis Books. I am immensely grateful to them for their friendly support and judicious advice. Without them this series would never have come together.

PHILIP SHELDRAKE
University of Durham

INTRODUCTION:
LIGHT THROUGH DARKNESS

The darkness is as the light to you. (Psalm 139)

The divine darkness is the inaccessible light.
(Dionysius the Areopagite)

TWO FORMATIVE MOMENTS

Two moments in my life encapsulate, in my mind and in my heart, the content of Orthodox thought and spirituality. They were neither particularly significant nor especially striking moments. Indeed, they were simple, even somber; they were routine and almost unnoticed. Yet these two experiences define the context within which I understand what it means to be an Orthodox Christian with a tradition spanning two thousand years. Curiously, both of these moments were incidents relating to loss. They involved two funerals. They were instances of a darkness that can be formative and transformative alike.

The first of these experiences occurred in the winter of 1979, during one of many visits to Mount Athos in my student years. This historical monastic republic lies on the northernmost peninsula of Greece and boasts twenty monasteries as well as numerous hermitages. The present book contains two chapters about the importance of silence and prayer as these draw upon Athonite spirituality. Chapter 5 explores the beginnings of monasticism; Chapter 6 describes more recent experiences that reveal an unbroken tradition.

I recall, then, journeying by foot through a deluge of stormy winter weather. I had travelled several hours during the night, accompanying an abbot, to attend the funeral of a monk, who had just passed away. That night, at an abandoned hermitage where we stopped to rest, the abbot celebrated liturgy in a tiny chapel that could fit no more than three or four people.

What impressed me the most was not the utter silence of the little church, the deep darkness of the still night, or even the solemn beauty of that memorable service. It was, rather, the sense that this church was overwhelmingly filled with a presence. There was a strong sense of the company of others – countless others, it seemed. It was so vividly clear to me that the two of us – the abbot and myself – were in fact the minority in that chapel, far fewer than the multitude that actually constituted, almost stiflingly crowded, the celebration of liturgy.

The second experience occurred some years later, in the fall of 1991, at the funeral service of the late Patriarch Demetrios, a leader still affectionately remembered for his softness and meekness. It seemed to me so fitting that it was during his tenure that the Orthodox Church worldwide was invited to dedicate a day of prayer for the protection of the environment, which we human beings have treated so harshly. Demetrios encouraged his faithful to walk gently on the earth, just as he did. Chapter 7 explores the unique Orthodox perspectives on the environment as well as the profound Orthodox principles behind ecological preservation.

Numerous religious and governmental heads attended the funeral of this beloved spiritual leader. This hardly surprised me. After all, as Ecumenical Patriarch, Demetrios was 'first among equals' of all Orthodox bishops. In this service, contrary to my earlier experience on Mount Athos, I expected capacity attendance.

What I was not prepared for, however, was the simplicity of the service itself. The solemnity and silence were truly remarkable, even refreshing. Indeed, were it not for the pres-

ence in the Patriarchal Church of St George of recognisable
religious leaders and notable secular representatives, nothing at all would have indicated the supreme honour of state
proportions due to this prelate.

There was nothing whatsoever extravagant about the
preparation or the commemoration. What was most extraordinary was that this funeral was typical of any other
funeral. It was so very, very ordinary. It occurred to me that
this could quite easily have been the funeral of any Orthodox
clergyman anywhere in the world. Demetrios lay in a simple
coffin, dressed as a bishop, yet more resembling a mere monk.

TWO FUNDAMENTAL ELEMENTS

Two fundamental elements of Orthodox spiritual thought are
quite apparent in these two personal moments. The first
experience betrays something of the aspect of *communion* in
Orthodox worship and practice. There is always much more
happening than that which is visible. There is constant communication and open communion with the past and with
those who have passed on. The present is never isolated,
never separated from the past or indeed from the future. It is
influenced by a historical tradition that includes – to quote
the Divine Liturgy of St John Chrysostom, quietly being celebrated in the tiny chapel on that cold, rainy night of 1979 –
'the prophets, apostles, preachers, martyrs, confessors, ascetics, and indeed every spirit of the righteous people of God'.
And it is informed by the heavenly kingdom that embraces –
to quote from the same liturgy – 'hosts of archangels, tens of
thousands of angels, the many-eyed cherubim and the six-
winged seraphim'. The liturgy, too, comprises an independent
chapter (Chapter 2), although it actually constitutes an integral part of every chapter. Moreover, the notion of spiritual
companionship and direction – a further, more personal element of communion – is explored in the final chapter
(Chapter 8).

The second experience denotes something of the dimension

of *martyrdom* that characterises Orthodox people and places. Persecutions and divisions have always marked the history of the Orthodox Church – not unlike the story of the early Christian Church. These have shaped Orthodox identity and Orthodox spirituality alike. Persecution has perpetually, persistently and profoundly proved fundamental and essential to the life of the Eastern Church. While it may not in fact be a normal feature of Christian life, martyrdom is definitely a normative factor of the Christian way. Martyrdom – whether a 'red martyrdom' of blood in the arena or a 'white martyrdom' of conscience in the heart – is undoubtedly part and parcel of the Orthodox way of living and thinking. Therefore, in many ways, the spiritual insights discovered when approaching the Church of the East are characterised and coloured by an element of darkness and brokenness.

This last point must be further 'unpacked'; for, the spirituality of the Christian East is often solely identified with particular characteristic elements: the emphasis on the vision of God as light, the richness of the liturgy as ritual, the beauty of the icons as God-visible, the negative dimension of theology as God-invisible, the way of perfection as deification, and the rigour of asceticism as discipline. All of these features certainly constitute important elements, which are either assumed implicitly or expressed emphatically throughout this book.

Yet, in many ways, the secret of Eastern Christian spirituality lies in that which is unseen and unheard. The depth of its spiritual teaching is discerned in its sense of mystery, which is always experienced paradoxically, and never simply understood philosophically. Hence, the vision of God is an encounter of light, but only in an awareness of the reality of darkness. The liturgy is an act of communion, but only after the recognition of human isolation and fragmentation. Icons reveal the divine face of God, but only when we have confessed the shattered image in ourselves and in our world. Deification is encountered as the way of perfection and salvation, but it is only experienced through the way of imperfection. And the rigour of ascetic discipline is not so much an exercise of human independence as a realisation of our dependence on God. The silent experience of God through the expression of tears is examined in Chapter 4.

By the same token, fundamental doctrines such as that of the Holy Trinity, while not the specific focus of attention in a separate chapter, are taken for granted, like the air that we breathe, in relation to Orthodox spirituality. Thus, Chapter 4 explains why God the Father is beyond all names; Chapter 2 examines the liturgy as the tangible presence and communion of Jesus Christ, the Son of God; while Chapter 8 explores the phenomenon of spiritual direction as a practical way of engendering men and women in the life of the Holy Spirit.

The deeper insight of Orthodox spirituality is that it always indicates a way of renunciation and surrender, rather than an alternative – mostly exotic, perhaps even impressive – way of success and achievement. It refuses to reduce God to manageable proportions, able to be comprehended and contained in chapters of a scholarly treatise. The life of the Spirit is certainly larger than our minds can include, always larger than our lives can imagine, and much larger than our world can contain. It is always known in darkness, 'seen as in a mirror, dimly' (1 Cor. 13:12). In this book, darkness is described as the only way to light, imperfection and brokenness as the only available forms of healing, despair as the only avenue leading to hope, and sin as the sole possibility of deification.

This book provides an introduction to another way of life, another way of seeing things, another way of spirituality. It considers and explores a selection of central and familiar themes of Orthodox spirituality, such as theology and asceticism, liturgy and monasticism, images and Easter, all of which embrace the fullness of this rich and varied tradition. *Light through Darkness* adopts as its unique focus and perspective the element of imperfection, brokenness and darkness as a celebration of the deifying, perfecting and illuminating presence of God in every aspect of the spiritual life. My hope is that it will serve as a background against which to appreciate Orthodox history (early, Byzantine, medieval and more contemporary) and spirituality (in its various cultural and national expressions).

INITIATION AND INSPIRATION

My purpose, then, is to accompany the reader inside an Orthodox church, allowing the reader to sit quietly and simply soak in the wisdom communicated by the wood and stones. Certainly, upon entering a traditional Orthodox church, one is immediately transported – by its very structure – to another reality, a world imbued with a richness of history and mystery that stretch backwards in time for over two thousand years and extend upwards in prayer to eternity.

I am neither an artist nor a mystic. I am a theologian and a deacon. As such, I have moved and worshipped within the walls of two chapels that comprise the heart of the theological institutions where I have taught. My experience of liturgy in the seminary Chapel of the St Andrew's Theological College in Sydney (Australia) and of Holy Cross School of Theology in Boston MA (USA) reflects in a silent and sacramental manner certain important principles of Orthodox architecture and art. These provide a basic initiation into an Orthodox world-view. They are an opportunity – or invitation – to enter the Orthodox church and just sit there, simply 'to be there'. These principles include:

- a sense of solemn mystery, highlighted by a darkness and quietness;
- colourful images around and above the worshipping community, inviting the faithful into the living company of saints;
- precious objects and relics, reflecting the light of flickering oil lamps and candles at the rise and setting of the sun;
- and, an elaborate liturgical ritual, with movement and song, transfiguring the entire interior.

The humblest Orthodox church, on even the most ordinary day of yearly cycle, will share in the majesty of this experience. It is a syn-aesthetic interplay of Byzantine architecture, sacred image and mystical prayer that witnesses to the possibility of only celestial comparison.

There is a well-known legend about an embassy sent by Prince Vladimir to Constantinople in the latter part of the tenth century in order to see whether the Russian people should adopt the religion of the Byzantines. After attending worship in the Great Church of Hagia Sophia, the envoys are said to have reported their overwhelming experience in the following words recorded in the *Russian Primary Chronicle*:

> We knew not whether we were in heaven or on earth, for surely there is no such splendor or beauty anywhere upon earth. We cannot describe it to you; we only know that God dwells there among people . . . We cannot forget that beauty.[1]

By modern Western standards, the Byzantine world would undoubtedly have seemed unfamiliar, perhaps even strange – it was a rigidly and intensely hierarchical society, almost obsessed with piety and ritual. Yet there is no question that Byzantine art and architecture were intimately connected, if not identified with the religious experience (both individual and communal) of the people, and this connection was variously and richly manifested in the diverse cultural expressions of Byzantium (Greek, Syriac, Coptic, Armenian, Georgian and Slavic). Russia ultimately accepted Orthodox Christianity based on this sacred reciprocity between religion and culture, between architecture and worship, as well as between mystery and beauty.

THEOLOGY, THEOSIS AND THEOPHANY

Byzantine architecture is fascinating in itself, but it is perhaps most intriguing for its 'otherness', its mysterious nature, its distance from the familiar. To Byzantine worshippers, as to their modern contemporaries, the church reflects God's dwelling-place. The building itself, and all that it contains, is a *theophany*, a manifestation of God's own beauty and wonder. Since the aim of Byzantine worship was the deification of all humanity and the sanctification of all creation, churches became the link between this world and another world. Whether a small community chapel in Greece, or a tiny rock-cave church in Cappadocia, or an enormous imperial cathedral in Constantinople, the focus and function always had a single purpose: to reveal the fullness of divine glory and heavenly splendour in this world as God's creation and abolish the man-made distinction between sacred and profane.

The church, then, is God's dwelling-place on earth. Every sound, sight and smell in an Orthodox church – the lamps, the bells, the icons, the vestments, the liturgical books and medieval chants – is an epiphany, an essential link between the heavenly and the terrestrial, the spiritual and material, soul and body. While, over the centuries, the altar – with all its clerical activity and hierarchical administration – became more inaccessible to the laity, the architecture of the church continued to emphasise and embrace all the people. This is quite literally true, as any visitor to an Orthodox church will observe. In the domed churches, especially popular since the sixth century, the centre of the building always reminded the community that not only was 'the kingdom of God . . . at hand' (cf. Matt. 3:2), but also that every minute detail of their lives, just as every speck of dust in the world, lay securely in the hands of the almighty God, the *Pantokrator*.

The reason that Orthodox Christians, much like their Byzantine forebears, can acknowledge this truth lies in a double doctrine that constitutes the very heart of their theology. It is the simultaneous affirmation of the absolute transcendence and immediate immanence of God. According to the spiritual teaching of the Orthodox Church, God is radically unknown and unknowable (in divine essence), while at the same time tangible and accessible (in divine energies).

As the Creator of all, the ground and source of all being, God is invisible, incorporeal, inaccessible, ineffable, inexpressible and indescribable. Such a teaching is often called *apophatic* or *negative theology*. It is the recognition that 'the true worshippers will worship the Father [not in any concrete place or material space, but] in spirit and truth' (John 4:23). This teaching is further developed in Chapter 3.

However, this is only half of the truth, one side alone of the doctrine. As the Creator of all, God is also totally manifest in all beings and in all things. All creation is the self-manifestation of God. Every detail in this world conceals the self-communication of God, 'present everywhere and filling all things' (from a daily Prayer to the Holy Spirit). Such a conviction is called *kataphatic* or *positive theology*.

These two theologies, the vision of God as darkness and light alike, resemble two sides of the same coin. To return to the architecture of an Orthodox church, the created materials on the wall as well as the human members inside the church – the wood and the brick, the stone and the marble, as well as the living faithful themselves – all 'become participants of divine grace' (St John of Damascus, eighth century), communicants of the One depicted on the images themselves.

ARCHITECTURE AND MYSTERY

The basic structure itself of a traditional Orthodox church is a synthesis of two classical elements: the dome (used as early as the fourth century) and the basilica (the earliest and simplest example of church architecture, built from available regional materials such as wood, stone and brick). Nevertheless, an Orthodox church is integrally and insistently three-dimensional. The church has three clearly defined spaces, three definite architectural zones. The dome is reserved for the image of Christ (or *Pantokrator*), the central feature that embraces and enlightens the entire building. The second space is the church proper (or *naos*), filled with images of the saints and martyrs, monks and married people alike, appearing almost to blend in with the congregation itself. The third zone is dedicated to the Virgin Mary (or *Theotokos*).

The dome is circular in shape, symbolical of the eternal and uncircumscribable divinity, a line without beginning or end. The floor plan of the church proper is rectangular, an image of the defined and limited nature of this world with its clear demarcations, beginnings and ends. The apse in the middle holds together the upper and lower zones, belonging to both and yet also pertaining to neither, uniting both the heavenly and the earthly realms, while at the same time inviting people to reconcile Creator and creation in their own bodies and in their surrounding world. The Mother of God, depicted in the apse, assumes both spherical and rectangular shape. She is the personification of this vocation and reconciliation. Thus, the apse reveals the sign and presence of God piercing history and entering time. In traditional churches, the absence of any pews further breaks down the separation between heaven and earth. Any subsidiary vaults and structural extensions assume the shape of a cross, the ultimate symbol of reconciliation and transfiguration (especially from the sixth-century reign of Justinian).[2]

Beyond the sense of mystery, the significance of imagery, and the sensitivity to liturgy, perhaps the greatest contribution of Byzantine architecture is flexibility. Orthodox architecture has endured the test of time, while also absorbing new techniques and building materials. It is at once traditional and original, always seeking to preserve the same essential dimensions.

Byzantine architecture followed fixed formulas and rigid regulations, particularly after the tenth century when there were few if any new structural developments, with the exception perhaps of exterior decorations and the addition of bell-towers. Nevertheless it always remained above all a responsive art, tending to assume cultural and regional styles, bequeathing to subsequent generations an architectural beauty of countless variations on the same theme. It is an art and an architecture that are aptly summed up in the

Greek word *philokalia* ('love of the beautiful').[3] It is a living tradition that, at least in its more genuine expressions, seeks to retain a delicate balance between the aesthetic and the ascetic, between beauty and simplicity, in the fragility and vulnerability of the material and ephemeral.

1. ORTHODOX SPIRITUALITY: RECLAIMING THE VOCABULARY, REFOCUSING THE VISION

The Word assumed flesh. (John 1:14)

I await the life of the age to come.
(Nicaean-Constantinopolitan Creed)

It would be helpful from the outset to offer certain terminological clarifications. When people use – and it is indeed now fashionable to do so – the term 'spirituality', whether with reference to Orthodox spirituality or generally, any number of meanings and moods are implied. There are those who adopt the term lavishly and quite loosely, often to the deterrence or even abhorrence of others who avoid the term completely. Some Orthodox theologians are quick to claim that there is no reference in the classical tradition to 'spirituality' or emphasise the connection between the Spirit of God and the spiritual life.

The truth is that the words 'spirituality' and 'spiritual' are dangerous, if only because as terms they are so vulnerable to misunderstanding and misuse. When we speak of a spiritual person, we generally mean it as a signpost; here is someone concerned with heavenly things alone, who sees only the mystical dimensions of the world. We might either idolise or else ignore such a person. Yet we rarely choose to identify ourselves with them. Meaning almost anything, the terms 'spirituality' and 'spiritual' mean almost nothing unless carefully nuanced.[1]

Our theological language is shaped very early in life. Unfortunately, after many years and numerous attempts by well-meaning adults, who teach us at Sunday school, who preach spiritual sermons or teach theological courses, we grow up to become either intent on or else content with fitting the vastness of the world and of God into small boxes of our own devising. So it is, then, that such words as 'spirituality' carry an enormous weight of baggage throughout history and our own life. It is a word that can project wrong cues and even cause much harm. The long struggle to sort out a genuine theological vocabulary has made me more aware of ways in which religious language can often strike a false note – the narcissistic babble that transforms itself into spirituality, the conventional 'language of a land with no known inhabitants'.[2]

Therefore, it is helpful to reclaim our theological vocabulary. And, if we have any guides in this endeavour, the Orthodox Church would claim that it is the saints of the Church, who teach us the process of learning and relearning what it is consciously to know and to reflect God's love in the world. The 'church of the fathers' has many inhabitants. And, in living with the saints, in realigning a genuine relationship with these men and women, we find that vocabulary comes to life and forces us to question and even to shed inadequate definitions that we have received from our childhood or our culture, which we have formed – perhaps deformed – as 'spiritual' means in order to justify our 'secular' ends.

The aim, ultimately, in any discussion about 'spirituality' is to bring about some form of reconciliation between the ways in which we understand our world and God. The goal is to bring healing to a world that has grown accustomed to an unholy dissociation between spirituality and morality, and to a disciplinary divorce within academia itself of Christian Ethics (in Protestant confessions), Moral Theology (in Roman Catholic circles) and Christian Spirituality (in Orthodox theology). Somehow, we are called to close the gap, to coincide the stress on fleeing from the world and the anxiety to change the world; to bring together the struggle towards personal holiness and the struggle towards social justice; to reconnect personal salvation and cosmic transformation.[3]

It is true that whenever we speak – whether about things in

heaven or on earth – we are drawing upon established, indeed presumed values of ourselves and of our world. Therefore, as I contemplate the term 'spirituality', I consider three concepts to be fundamental and formative. These three concepts serve as my basis for drawing connections between Orthodox spirituality and the world around us. I approach these terms with a proper sense of humility before the great mystery of language – that human venture which begins with the ear and tongue of an infant, proceeds through the joys and tensions that define the relationship between our words and those of others, and finally reaches for the very mystery of God's Word.

In this introductory chapter, I would like to concentrate on these three fundamental terms and concepts, so central to any understanding of Orthodox spirituality or of its intrinsic value today, as a humble attempt to translate an old faith into a new language.

ESCHATOLOGY: 'DYING, YET BEHOLD WE LIVE'

'I await the life of the age to come,' proclaims the Orthodox 'symbol of faith', otherwise known as the Nicaean-Constantinopolitan Creed, formulated in the fourth century and recited at each celebration of the Divine Liturgy. In theological jargon, talk about 'the age to come' is known as 'eschatology', the study of the last events (or, *eschata*). Most of us assume that the last times and the last things imply some apocalyptic or escapist attitude towards the world. It took a long time for theologians to realise that eschatology is not the last, perhaps unnecessary chapter in some tedious manual or course of dogmatics. Eschatology is not the teaching about what *follows* everything else in this world and in these times. It is the teaching about *our relationship* to those last things and last times. In essence, it is about the last-ness and the lasting-ness of all things. The Omega gives meaning to the Alpha; this world is interpreted in light of the age to come.

However, it was my friends in the early desert of Egypt and Palestine who would later plunge me all unwitting into the essence of eschatology. That dry desert, from the middle of the third century until around the end of the sixth century, became a laboratory for exploring hidden truths about heaven and earth, as well as a forging ground for drawing connections between the two. The hermits who inhabited that desert tested and studied what it means to be human – with all the tensions and temptations, all of the struggle beyond survival, all of the contact with good and the conflict with evil. And on their course, some of them made many mistakes; others made fewer mistakes. Whoever said that there is a clear and simple answer to the questions of life? Yet, these men and women dared to push the limits; they challenged and defied the norms of what was acceptable in their age and society.

I think I received further insights into some of the deeper dimensions of eschatology when I faced my own mortality in the brokenness of my son's cerebral palsy. The word 'eschatology' no longer seemed other-worldly to me; it did not focus exclusively on future events. I was faced with the vulnerability of an infant – an intense experience of a child so intricately caught up in the last things. The lie about heaven being elsewhere split wide open; and this could only occur after I had admitted that I was really broken.

What is far more difficult, it seems, and far more important than learning to live, is learning to die. Once we sense that we are in the shadow of God, then we discover light, so much light that our vision of the world improves dramatically. Then we know that holiness is near. Dying and loss are lessons in how to live and how to love.

So our spiritual reflections are fatally flawed if they do not begin with the reality of the cross, with the suffering and cries of those deeply affected and directly threatened by the legacy of the cross. An eschatological interpretation of the world introduces a raw criticism of our struggle for survival, of power dynamics and human domination. It recognises that what is personal and private is also political and public. An eschatological vision of reality and the world also offers a way out of the impasse of provincialism and the evil of confessionalism. It reflects our refusal to acquiesce – whether out of innocence or ignorance or intimidation, whether by choice or by force.

Ultimately, eschatology is our hope against all hopelessness. It is our *silent conviction* that our efforts on this planet are not ours alone, never limited to what we can achieve, but that the Source and End of all life is working in us, through us and above us for the well-being of all creation, including our tiny part in it.

SILENCE: LISTENING TO THE WORLD

What is far more difficult and far more important than learning to speak is learning to be silent. As a father of two teenagers, I know that silence is not the absence of noise but the ability to discern between the two. It is the power and wisdom of learning to listen. Such listening is surely the prerequisite for any silence. Thus, silence is active, alive and affectionate. It resembles a spider spinning its web, or a silkworm creating its silk. It reminds us to take our soul with us wherever we go.

In the desert of Egypt, silence was described as the daughter of patience, the mother of watchfulness. When all words are abandoned, a new awareness arrives. Silence awakens us from numbness to the world around us, from our dullness of vision.

> Abba Poemen said: 'Be watchful inwardly; but be watchful also outwardly.'[4]

For the early desert dwellers, silence is a requirement of life, the first duty of love. Silence is a way of waiting, a way of watching, a way of noticing – and not ignoring – what is going on in our heart and in our world. It is the glue that binds our attitudes and our actions, our belief and our behaviour. Silence reflects our surrender to God as well as to new patterns of learning and living. When we are silent, we learn by suffering and undergoing, not just by speculating and understanding. Silence confirms our readiness to lead a counter-cultural way of life, to choose rather than to be led, to admit our limited perspective as possessors and consumers, and to appreciate another, unlimited perspective of 'life in abundance' (John 10:10).

What we learn in silence is that we are all intimately interconnected, all mutually interdependent.

> Suppose we were to take a compass [says Dorotheus of Gaza in the sixth century] and insert the point and draw the outline of a circle. The center point is the same distance from any point on the circumference ... Let us suppose that this circle is the world and that God is the center; the straight lines drawn from the circumference to the center are the lives of human beings . . . The closer these are to God, the closer they come to each other and to the world; and the closer they come to each other and to the world, the closer they become to God.[5]

The truth is that all things are so intimately interrelated, cohering in each other beyond our imagination. Nothing living is self-contained. There is no autonomy – only a distinction between a sense of responsibility and a lack thereof. The result of any bifurcation between spirituality and reality is inevitably catastrophic.

DETACHMENT: THE VALUE OF ACTION

Finally, the early ascetics deeply valued 'detachment'. For us, detachment is a concept that has lost its positive connotation. Nowadays, it is used in a negative sense, to mean perhaps the opposite of a healthy engagement with the world and with other people. It conveys a sense of aloofness, a studied remoteness that implies lack of concern. Yet the monastic interpretation of detachment could not be more different. In the desert, detachment meant not allowing either worldly values or self-centredness to distract us from what is most essential in our relationship with God and with our world.

Dorotheus of Gaza describes detachment as being free from

forcing certain things to happen. It is faith sufficiently strong as to be thoroughly realistic in its encounter with the world. It is paying close attention to details, even to the intake of food and the acquisition of possessions. Not in order to punish ourselves, but in order to discern the value of sharing, the presence of suffering and the intrinsic honour of good things in life. This sort of detachment is neither passive nor remote; paradoxically, it is fully engaged with the world. It is a prayer that can absorb all manner of pain and transform it into hope.

For the early desert elders, detachment from everything and everyone only underlined the dignity of everything and everyone. Detachment was the first step of monastic renunciation or of the flight to the desert. Moreover, it was more than merely spatial or material.

> Abba Zosimas always liked to say: 'It is not possessing something that is harmful, but being attached to it.'[6]

Detachment is not the inability to focus on things, material or other; it is precisely the spiritual capacity to focus on all things, material *and* other, without any dependence or attachment. It is primarily, then, something spiritual, an attitude of life.

In this respect, detachment is ongoing, demanding continual refinement over years of practice. The desert elders speak of stages in the way of detachment, just as there are steps in the spiritual 'ladder of divine ascent'.[7] Detachment resembles the shedding of a number of coats of skin, until our senses are sharpened, or until – as one desert father put it – 'our inner vision becomes keen'.[8] When we learn what to let go of, we also learn what is worth holding on to. Think of it in this way: it is simply not possible to share something precious, or even to hold a lover's hand, when our fists are clenched, holding tightly onto something. The purpose of monastic detachment is not to teach us how to live apart from the social world, but to inspire us all about how to live within the world as a responsible part of society. Detachment is an expression of love, a positive energy that must be incarnated into action.

The same attitude extends beyond one's connection with other people to one's relationship to material things.

> Abba Agathon was once walking with his disciples. One of them, on finding a small green pea on the road, said to the old man: 'Father, may I take it?' The old man, looking at him with astonishment, replied: 'Was it you that put it there?' 'No,' said the brother. 'How then,' continued the old man, 'can you take up something, which you did not put down?'[9]

The detachment recommended here is a form of letting go. We are to let go of our actions, of our words, and finally of our life. The aim of letting go is the learning of true prayer, the starting-point and ending-point of all action. By letting go, we learn to pray spontaneously, a gift that children seem to have innately, but which takes a lifetime for us to recover as adults. And in this kind of prayer, the way of silence and the way of service coincide.

> Abba Poemen said: 'If three people meet, of whom the first fully preserves interior peace, the second gives thanks to God in illness, and the third serves with a pure mind, these three are doing the same work.'[10]

Work is never separated from prayer. Rather, prayer frees us for carefree service of others, where we are no longer conditioned by the burden of necessity but always prepared for the novelty of grace. Just as silence conditions our words, prayer too conditions our works. Detachment signifies humility, and humility looks to shift the focus of oneself as the centre of the world and to place oneself in the service of others. The humble person is always satisfied, always shares, always gives, always gives thanks.

A truly detached person cannot tolerate creating miserable poverty for the sake of accumulating exorbitant wealth. The moral crisis of our global economic injustice is integrally spiritual; it signals something terribly amiss in our relationship with God, with people and with things. Yet, insulated as we are by privilege and by the sin of attachment, so many of us remain blind to the ecological devastation created by current global trade and investment regimes. The detached person is free, uncontrolled by attitudes that violently abuse the world, uncompelled by ways that simply use the world.

CONCLUSION

Walking the way of the heavenly kingdom, assuming the power of silence and recognising the value of detachment is to regain a sense of wonder, to be filled again with a sense of goodness, of God-liness. It is to recognise all things in God and to remember God in all things. Letting go and letting God – in a renewed eschatological attitude and a refreshing silence of love – is the crucial balance for our patterns of control. Keeping silence is at once a critical skill and channel for noticing the impact and effect of our actions.

Emptiness, then, in our language and our lifestyle provides the necessary corrective to our wastefulness in our words and our wealth. Here is a case when the darkness, or absence, becomes a beacon of hope and light. When through silence and detachment we learn to share, the spiritual world is anything but disconnected from the 'real' world. Then, the real world becomes one with the heavenly reality, which must be infused upon and inform this world. Then, we no longer lead lives disengaged from the injustice in our world. Then, our vision becomes enlarged, able to contain so much more than our selves or our own. Indeed, our heart is then able 'to contain the Uncontainable'.[11] Whenever we embrace such a cosmic vision, we cease to narrow life to our own concerns, our own desires and our own selves, attending in the process to our vocation to transform the entire creation of God. This is precisely the basis of Orthodox spirituality. And it is precisely the purpose of the Orthodox Liturgy.

2. LITURGY AND SACRAMENT:
THE WAY OF GRATITUDE AND GLORY

Christianity is a liturgical religion ... Worship comes first. (Georges Florovsky)

Liturgy is ... the joy of expectation and the expectation of joy. (Alexander Schmemann)

INTRODUCTION TO ANOTHER WORLD

The Notion of Tradition

In the Orthodox Church, devotional forms and gestures have been meticulously preserved for centuries without any significant change. This means that an Orthodox Christian entering a church for liturgy in the twenty-first century has every reason to believe, and is perhaps even able to perceive, that he or she is sharing the very same experience as the Byzantines did in the tenth century.

This powerful and pervasive aroma of antiquity and continuity will certainly impress Western Christians entering an Orthodox church for the first time. Orthodoxy typically presents – and is frequently so presented by its adherents – as a seamless robe, a totality in which every part adheres to the whole in primordial and perfect harmony. In actual fact, the attachment to *tradition* does not imply rigid immobility or stagnation. There has always been growth and development in Orthodox liturgy. The change may be slow, almost imperceptible, but this is because it is a natural process, never a reform imposed from above or programmed from below. We like to call it a *living* tradition. 'Of course it results in any number of loose ends, hard to reconcile practices, customs that overlap or even contradict one another; but they are loose ends of the living, rather than the well ordered immobility of the dead.'[1]

The question of course is how Orthodox liturgy will be retrieved and revealed not as merely emotional but as deeply essential, not as externally attractive but as essentially theological; for, it must be admitted that Orthodoxy is occasionally successful on the wrong grounds: because it is 'spiritually' exotic and esoteric, perhaps even escapist, or else sufficiently 'different'. People are attracted – sometimes distracted – by the orientalism of the music or the mysticism. Orthodox themselves are often enticed by the symbolical paraphernalia, by the explanation of every detail and gesture preserved over centuries.

Yet, liturgy is ultimately symbolical of only one thing, 'the one thing that alone is necessary' (Luke 10:42). The unique purpose of liturgy is the entrance into the kingdom of heaven. The liturgy is neither primarily ceremonial nor mystical. It is the mystical celebration and deeper conviction that 'Christ is in our midst'. Verse and voice are ultimately and intimately linked with this vision.

The liturgy, then, is *more than* a mere remembrance of acts and words of the Lord. Indeed, by analogy, tradition too is *more than* the mere remembrance of certain acts or words of Christ. It is precisely during the liturgy that Christ is transmitted, handed down to us (the literal sense of the Latin term *trado*). Orthodox spirituality would affirm the words of Irenaeus, that 'our whole life should conform to the Eucharist, and the Eucharist should confirm our whole life'.[2] There is, in this context, a virtual identity between Christ and tradition, between Christ as past, present and future (cf. Rev. 4:8).

Tradition, Liturgy and Doctrine

Tradition raises a further dimension in regard to the influence of *doctrinal development* on the liturgy. Imperial patronage in the early fourth century had profound consequences for the Church and its worship. The fourth century was a period of fierce doctrinal conflict and unprecedented theological creativity. 'Homoousian' and 'hypostasiac' terminology, christological and trinitarian theology; these discussions inevitably and indelibly left their mark also on Eastern liturgy. Moreover, an added prominence and prestige in liturgical matters was gradually concentrated on the imperial city of New Rome, Constantinople, whose *typikon* (or ritual) increasingly became 'typ-ical' for the whole of the Eastern Church.

No wonder, then, that liturgy is respected like doctrine in the minds of the Orthodox, that the *lex orandi* is so closely connected to the *lex credendi*. It is not difficult to appreciate why Byzantines of old and Orthodox today feel that: 'Truly, till heaven and earth pass away, not an iota, not a dot, would pass from the law' (Matt. 5:18) of liturgy. As John of Damascus, the eight-century champion of icons, wrote about tradition, 'we do not change the everlasting boundaries which our fathers have set, but we keep the tradition, just as we received it,'[3] so Nicholas Cabasilas, the fourteenth-century liturgical commentator, could write of liturgy, 'Beyond this it is not possible to go, nor can anything be added to it.'[4]

There are certain 'silent' doctrines, never formally defined, which are nonetheless maintained with as much inner conviction by the Orthodox Church as any explicit dogmatic formulation. As Basil of Caesarea wrote in the fourth century: 'Some things we have from written teaching, while others we have received from the apostolic tradition handed down to us in mystery; yet both of these have the same force for piety.'[5] The liturgy belongs to one of those powerful traditions *'handed down to us in mystery'*. This is why no one will blink an eye when the deacon – apparently out of nowhere, but certainly with a sense of profound apostolic conviction – stands in the middle of the church and cries out aloud, immediately preceding the recital of the Nicaean-Constantinopolitan Creed (known as 'the symbol of faith'):

'The doors! The doors! Wisdom! Let us be attentive!' This cry recalls the early days when the church's entrance was jealously guarded – out of fear for persecution during the first Christian period; out of fear for profanation in later centuries. Only the initiated members – those baptised and able to recite the common principles of belief – could remain in the church. No one moves today; certainly no one leaves. Yet, it remains another powerful, albeit silent reminder of the intimate link between credal formulation and liturgical adoration.

'My World and Yours' – Contrasts and Comparisons

Attending an Orthodox liturgy is like entering a world with a distinct architecture, a peculiar iconography, and even a remote altar space.[6] Ritual and richness abound here. The faithful do not see the full altar; the *prothesis* (or special table) where the gifts are prepared – without any obvious participation by the laity – is entirely out of sight.

Solemnity is the key here, not simplicity. Solemnity is the definition of the Eastern celebration of the Eucharist. The same may be said generally of liturgical space, movement and dress. In addition, there is an air of reverence, coupled with an atmosphere of informality. Therefore, the congregation is for the most part silent. Yet, they do not only worship with voice. They also worship with their eyes and ears. They will even worship with their body – moving about, lighting candles, standing, kneeling, making the sign of the cross at any time and many times, bowing or fully prostrating. They worship as well with their sense of smell – there is an abundance of incense, bread, oil and candles.

Surprisingly, not all – indeed sometimes very few – will approach for communion, although everyone lines up for the *antidoron* (the blessed bread) distributed at the conclusion of the service. Moreover, while the basic liturgical structure may be familiar, other features differ. There is less emphasis on the 'ministry of the word', there are lengthy litanies, two central processions or entrances, the readings are sung, a sermon is not crucial, the kiss of peace is often exchanged only among clergy, significant prayers are read 'silently' (or 'mystically' – in fact the most central prayer, the *anaphora*, may be as inaudible as the priest saying it is invisible), and communion is given with a spoon to adults and babies alike.

There is a sense in which two services appear to be going on at the same time – one within the sanctuary, and the other more visibly. The two coincide at some points, but in many ways the people in the congregation resemble only passive attendants. This idea of two liturgies, however, the celebration of liturgy on two levels, is symbolical of another twofold reality. It is a reminder that, in liturgy, heaven and earth somehow coincide; in some very real way, the two concelebrate. So let us now turn our attention to this profound symbolism.

'BLESSED IS THE KINGDOM'

The Liturgy as Heaven

When the liturgy appeared as a literary text in the East towards the end of the fourth century, the community was still mindful as much of Christ's second coming as of his passion and resurrection. The already acute sense of eager expectation was always heightened for the early Christians when they gathered for the eucharistic meal but it was particularly intensified during periods of persecution.[7] The Eucharist was an image of the heavenly banquet. So the early Christians looked two ways: forwards and backwards, or upwards and downwards; there was a keen sense of *anamnesis* (remembering the past) and *anaphora* (referring to the future). Here then, already adumbrated, is a double emphasis on liturgy as both heaven and home, or on home as heaven. The future kingdom was always a present reality, never a distant hope, and the Eucharist was a tangible foretaste of that kingdom.

The paradox of 'homeliness' and 'mysteriousness' is already

apparent in the second-century theological descriptions. This is certainly the case in the East, although the West seems early on to have preferred images of sacrifice to models of thanksgiving. Thus, while Irenaeus of Lyons (who came from Asia Minor to the West) emphasised the Eucharist as an offering of thanks, the prevailing view in the West belonged to Cyprian, who emphasised that the sacrifice offered in the rite was the passion of Christ. We must of course always be wary of simplistic distinctions; there are certainly exceptions to the rule. Thus, in the mid-fourth century, Cyril of Jerusalem also underlines the propitiatory character[8] and introduces into Eastern liturgy and spirituality a pious element, together with a language of fear with regard to the sacrament of Eucharist itself.

Over time, formerly simple or practical movements assumed significant and symbolical value. Thus, while the third-century Syrian document, *Didascalia Apostolorum*,[9] described the deacons' ministerial role as matter of fact, in the same century, the great Alexandrian thinker Origen developed an entire theology of Christian mystery and symbolism. This was continued by liturgical interpreters, such as Dionysius the Areopagite in the fifth century, Maximus the Confessor in the seventh, Germanos of Constantinople in the eighth, Theodore the Studite in the ninth, Symeon the New Theologian in the tenth, Nicholas and Theodore of Andida in the eleventh, Nicholas Cabasilas in the fourteenth, and Symeon of Thessalonika in the fifteenth century. Simple gestures assume solemn, even somber meaning:

> The deacons bring out the oblation, which they arrange and place on the awe-inspiring altar, a vision . . . awe-inspiring even to the onlookers. In the symbols we must see Christ, who is now being led to his passion and laid out on the altar . . . When the offering is brought out in the sacred vessels, the patens and chalices, you must think that Christ the Lord is coming out, led by the invisible host of ministers . . . (Deacons) wave their

fans . . . because the Body lying there is truly Lord by its union with the divine nature. With great fear it must be laid out, viewed and guarded . . . in fear, prayer and utter silence.[10]

The Liturgy as Home

Nevertheless, when Orthodox Christians enter the liturgy, it more than often appears that they are entering *the familiar surroundings of their home*. There is a sense of homeliness and informality. Indeed, people generally behave inside the church much as they behave outside. There is no sharp division between sacred and secular here. Instead, there is much movement: people drifting in and out, lighting candles, kneeling or bowing, venerating icons or making the sign of the cross, even talking. In the fourth century, John Chrysostom complained: 'Here in church, there is great disturbance and confusion, and it is as bad as a tavern. There is so much laughing and chattering.'[11]

To the outsider, Orthodox liturgy may well portray this air of informality and familiarity. Yet, this physicality and familiarity are an important part of Orthodox worship. Everything is material and real. The bread is always actual bread; the wine is bright and red, and it signifies not just death and sacrifice, but life and celebration. Baptism is full immersion; confession involves physical contact with the laying on of the hand. There is bread and oil and boiled wheat. The patristic principle that 'what is not assumed is not healed'[12] is very tangible here.

The liturgy becomes the ground on which all things meet and make sense, and outside of which everything remains unrecognisable and isolated. Within this powerful and pervading sense of home-ness and famili-arity, Orthodox bring to church food and drink prepared at home. They are 'participants at a festive meal', sharers of a banquet. They are not merely consumers; they are first and foremost worshippers. Prior to communion, the following prayer is recited: 'The lamb of God is broken and distributed; broken yet not divided; forever eaten yet never consumed; sanctifying those who partake.'

There is an important message here for a consumer age like ours. The liturgical ethos reverses the socially accepted norm. Our primary purpose and spiritual calling is not to struggle in a world where 'only the fittest survive'. Rather, we are invited to share, to be vulnerable, in accordance with the words of Christ at the Last Supper: 'Take, eat of this my body; drink of this, all of you, this is my blood.' These words are more than the institution of a sacrament; they are an inspiration of a new way of life.

In the liturgy we breathe the clean, unpolluted air of the resurrection. When the witness of the Revelation wrote 'I, John, was in the Spirit on the Lord's day . . . and I saw a new heaven and a new earth' (Rev. 1:10), he was actually saying, 'I, John, was in liturgy.' John the Divine thus becomes the forerunner of Eastern/Byzantine liturgical commentators. He recognised and revealed that everything makes sense and assumes full meaning in the liturgy.

In liturgy, then, we Orthodox feel at home and speak our mother tongue – the language of reconciliation and love. We know that God exists because we are embraced warmly and accepted unconditionally. We care for others because we discover them and discern their needs. We grow more sensitive to the 'groans and pains' of creation (Rom. 8:22) because everything is valued and inspired. The only valid response is gratitude and grace; these are, after all, the deeper meaning of the term 'eucharist'. And the only dissonant note in liturgy is disconnection and ingratitude.

We learn to share and to thank: for the sun and for the stars, for the pain and the tears, for the trees and the flowers, for the trials and the failures, for life and for death, for life's 'stuff'. This is why the liturgy begins from the moment when we leave home, when we are on our way to constitute the Church. It begins from the time the doors of the church are opened; or, as a friend of mine likes to say, when 'the church is prayed open'. There is no single 'moment' when the prayer of liturgy commences and no particular 'time' when it concludes. I wonder whether this is why Orthodox feel free to arrive late, or to come and go.

Heaven on Earth

This is the depth of the liturgy. It is the presence of angels, archangels, the kingdom of heaven, earth and its people, the whole of creation, and the Creator too. It is an all-embracing drama, a meeting-place of the earthly and the heavenly. This truth is made plain during the Small Entrance, when the following prayer is recited: 'Make with our entry an entry of your holy angels, celebrating the liturgy with us.' 'In this mystery,' the liturgy continues in the Great Entrance, 'we are icons of the cherubim.' Indeed, as John Chrysostom elsewhere affirms: 'Those in heaven and those on earth form a single festival, a shared thanksgiving, one choir.'[13]

To the outsider, one of the most striking qualities of Orthodox liturgy may well be the opulent ritualism, at least when contrasted to the apparent verbalism of other liturgies. Everything is always sung in the liturgy of the Orthodox. It might be said that Orthodox Christians do not come to church simply to pray. Nor do they go to church to be in silence. Something is happening there, in liturgy, and Orthodox Christians are invited to participate. Sometimes, I wonder whether Orthodox themselves are aware of this liturgical depth in their tradition. Perhaps it is of little importance. After all, how many of those who enjoy dancing would realise the historical origins or cultural background of that dance? Surely this hardly detracts from the personal joy and powerful experience of shared celebration and song.

Before each liturgy, Sunday by Sunday, Orthodox Christians pray: 'God, our God, who sent your heavenly bread, the food of the whole world, to bless us, bless also the offering.' Orthodox Christians assemble in liturgy to eat and to enjoy together, and not just to see and hear and feel the Word of God.[14]

'LET US GIVE THANKS TO THE LORD'

The Liturgy as Communion

The communal aspect of worship is central to the Orthodox mindset. There is a deep sense of belonging, within which one continues to preserve one's personal rhythm. So, upon entering church, we Orthodox do not pray alone. Instead, we light a candle before an icon – an image of the heavenly 'cloud of witnesses' – and place it alongside all the other lit candles.

The liturgy is not the sum of the gathered individuals. It is never a loose collection of people with some restricted parish plan, diocesan programme, church policy or religious vision. It is the freedom and space, where everyone journeys freely, each sails at will and chooses personally. The liturgy confirms personal hopes and dreams, although never of course at the expense or exclusion of others. The liturgy broadens our horizons and interests.

There is ample room; no presence is stifling or discomforting. Everyone crowds around the altar: 'Hosts of archangels, tens of thousands of angels, the many-eyed cherubim and the six-winged seraphim . . . the prophets, apostles, preachers, martyrs, confessors, ascetics', the living and the dead, the young and old, male and female, conservatives and liberals, sane and insane, healthy and unhealthy, rich and poor, powerful and vulnerable, educated and illiterate, religious and agnostic. They're *all* there! They *all* fit. Yet, at the same time, there is a unique place for each of them individually. This was precisely my experience on Mount Athos during that winter of 1979. It is also the breadth of the Greek word for reconciliation or forgiveness: *syn-choresis* literally implies 'being together in one place, sharing the same space'. We are never alone in liturgy; we are always with others, countless others:

in the company of angels, in the communion of saints, and in the comfort of all creation.

In liturgy, therefore, we learn to love. We understand that we are not mechanical pieces of a political machine, individuals in an anonymous society. We have a personal ministry in the mystery of life, valued for who and what we are. In this experience of eucharistic communion, Christ is formed in us; 'God makes of us a home' (John 14:23). How can such a liturgy grow old or stagnate? Upon leaving the liturgy, we are a grain of mustard seed, a kind of leaven, enthusiastic witnesses, a dynamic presence to the kingdom in the world.

The Liturgy as Mission

So inspired, we can 'depart in peace'. We move out once again to the same routine, to our respective work. Yet we now know otherwise; we now see differently. 'What was from the beginning, what we have heard, what we have seen with our eyes, what we have looked at and touched with our hands, concerning the word of life, this we declare . . . so that you also may have fellowship with us . . . and our joy may be complete' (1 John 1:1–4).

The goodness of God is celebrated and proclaimed; it results in the godliness and gladness of all creation. At the Small Entrance, the prayer begins: 'O Master and Lord . . . grant us to glorify your goodness.' There is nothing to add to this experience, nothing else to express. In mind-blowing words that are often missed, the deacon again stands in the centre of the church and exclaims: 'Let us stand in goodness. Let us stand with awe.' It is not a call to be upstanding or awake. It is a reminder of the radical reversal of secular values brought about in the liturgy. As one Orthodox theologian puts it, the deacon is saying, 'Don't just do something; *stand* there!' Again in the words of the Orthodox liturgy, 'Standing in the temple of your glory, we think we are in heaven.' This is a reminder of the apostolic sentiment on the Mountain of Transfiguration: 'Lord, it is good to be here' (Matt. 17:4).

The crucial question then is not what happens to the elements or what happens to the individuals who may or may not be present, but what happens to the entire Church and to the whole of creation. The liturgy is never for inner consumption but always for cosmic transfiguration.

The Liturgy as Prayer

The prayer of the Orthodox Church was not shaped primarily within pious hearts of individual saints or formulated originally within the libraries of historical monasteries. It was fundamentally formed in the liturgy of the worshipping community. The liturgy provided the regular and rhythmical pattern for both adoration and intercession. The public cycle of weekly liturgies and the unceasing invocation of the Name of Jesus were always intimately connected, like blood cells in a body. Morning praise, evening thanksgiving and Sunday Eucharist – together, these marked the hours of human activity and sealed the presence of God in the life of the community. Every instant of time, just as every detail of the world, was rejuvenated by contact with the fire of liturgical prayer. All of the services collectively, and each office uniquely, prophetically preached and tangibly revealed the signs of the kingdom.

The liturgy, therefore, guides each worshipper beyond his or her own individual concerns, embracing every soul, every city and every century. In liturgy, I hear not just the voice of my own supplication but the echo of the voice of the Apostles, the Martyrs, the Fathers and Mothers, the theologians, the poets, the teachers, the missionaries, the ascetics 'and of every spirit' through the ages. And together with the prayer of each of these, my own personal prayer is called to join spontaneously in a joyful act of at-one-ment and oneness. Others can pray for me. However, no one else can pray in my place.

In liturgy, after much care and effort, my prayer becomes attuned to the prayer of the whole world, not unlike the tuning of a musical instrument. With much toil and struggle, within my own soul, a synthesis is brought about with the soul of the world. No wonder that Orthodox liturgy appears endless.

'NEW HEAVEN AND NEW EARTH'

The Liturgy as Cosmic

The emphasis above on 'goodness' gives rise to a final point about the liturgy, and is reminiscent of yet another scriptural passage: 'God saw everything that was made, and indeed it was very good' (Gen. 1:31).

Like the concept of spirituality itself, it is so easy to misinterpret the purpose of liturgy as encouraging escape from this world. We all know that the world should not be regarded as a mere or useful necessity; we all admit that we should live in modest harmony with nature, not in audacious supremacy over it. Yet, we are inexorably trapped in the stifling circle of our individual desires. Well, the liturgy is supposed to transform the entire world, to the least of our brothers and sisters, as well as to the last speck of dust. It is never an escape from all this; instead, it gives us a refreshing sense of *enlarged* life.

The entire world becomes the space of the liturgy. So we pray for people in all circumstances and needs: 'for the sick, the suffering, the needy, those traveling, for those in captivity', and 'for the whole world, for the parish, every parish, for every city and land, and for the faithful who dwell in them'. There is a mosaic in Ravenna portraying saints, martyrs, hierarchs and faithful laity, each of them holding a crown that they will place at the feet of Christ. Similarly, before the liturgy, the priest places the 'lamb' (a piece of bread representing the body of Christ) at the centre of the *diskos* (signifying the disk of the world), surrounding it with fragments of bread symbolising the Mother of God, the angels, prophets and saints, as well as all of the dead and the living.

Together, heaven and earth offer one hymn, one prayer, one feast and one doxology.[15] Everything sings and exclaims, 'crying aloud and saying: holy, holy, holy'. Everything aspires to divine holiness and symbolises an overture to paradise. The created world does not escape to heaven; indeed, the whole world becomes an organic part of the mystery of heaven.[16] Within that context, one diminishes in humility and offers thanksgiving and glorification for all.

The Dimension of Personal Prayer

While liturgy is not identical to prayer, it is nonetheless a part of prayer. And, while prayer is not identified with liturgy, it cannot be understood apart from liturgy. Prayer accompanies every aspect and detail of life, including liturgy, while liturgy becomes the context within which the contour of prayer is revealed. Moreover, liturgy is not a public or corporate form of prayer. It is of course a gathering for prayer, but it is much more than that. Liturgy is work; it is 'the work of the people' (the literal meaning of the Greek term *leitourgia*).

Therefore, as we have already observed, the primary purpose of liturgy is not to pray. Rather, liturgy aims at gathering together – in one and the same place, as well as 'in one and the same mind' – the people of God, the communion of the saints, as the body of Christ. It is the sacrament where the Church becomes what it is supposed, indeed called, to be.[17] It is the mystery that constitutes the very essence of the Church (cf. Matt. 16:18). In liturgy, an Orthodox Christian knows that he or she is never lonely, that 'one Christian is no Christian' (Tertullian), that no one is saved alone. In liturgy, then, we are always in the presence of Christ. It is 'the Lord who acts' and we who adore; it is God who reaches out and we who respond.

While, then, we may be able to pray alone, no one can celebrate the liturgy alone. The liturgy never looks primarily to personal piety or spiritual progress. Rather, it aims at bearing one another's burdens, at loving one another, 'even as we have been loved' (John 13:34). The liturgy – both by gift and by grace – is an initiation into the sacred and sanctifying relationship enjoyed by the Father, the Son and the Holy Spirit.

Prayer, nonetheless, accompanies every detail and dimension of our life. And so, in liturgy, we make petitions and offer intercessions in prayer. We unite our will and our mind, our word and our mouth, our problems and our priorities, as well as our emotions and our passions, with the very content and ultimate intent of liturgy, namely 'the life of the world' (John 6:51). We submit ourselves to the will of God, so that God's will may 'be done on earth as it is in heaven' (the Lord's Prayer).

Each of us attends with different sins, different circumstances and different suffering. Yet all of us are called to 'be attentive' to what is really happening, until we are completely transformed, until God is forcefully 'beseeched and invoked and implored [during the most sacred moment of Liturgy!] to send down the Holy Spirit upon us and upon the gifts that we have brought, in order to make of these the body and blood of our Lord and God and Savior Jesus Christ. Amen.'

The Iconic Dimension

The vision and boundaries of the world are, therefore, far broader than the limited space and life of any human being. I may be the centre of this vision or theophany, but through liturgy I become aware that I am also but a detail of the world. Indeed, the world ceases to be something that I observe objectively and becomes something of which I am a part personally. I no longer feel that I am a stranger (whether threatened or threatening); I am now a friend in and of the world. How sadly Christians have misinterpreted the words of Christ that we are *in* but not *of* the world (cf. John 17:14, 16).

In liturgy, an iconic understanding of the world prevails. In this perspective, the 'other' world penetrates and permeates 'this' world, and the eternal infests and invests the historical. Nothing is ever profane within this vision; nothing whatsoever is neutral. Everything is an icon revealing God and indicates a way to God. The whole world is a 'cosmic liturgy', as

Maximus the Confessor professed in the seventh century. The liturgy ultimately confesses and only celebrates what is already truly there, though often neither clearly perceived nor fully practised.

We have already noted that, when an Orthodox Christian enters the church, he or she is entering the comfort of his or her own home. We may further clain that, when they leave the church, they are still in the liturgy because the whole world is a sacrament. The whole world resembles a liturgy unleashed. Perhaps our 'original sin' lies in our failure or refusal to view life and the world as a sacrament of communion with God. The liturgy restores the balance of communion in our world.

The liturgy transforms the world, although this does not always imply conforming to the world. The liturgy is not a compromise with this world; rather, it is a promise of the world to come. It is the showering of a divine light that is avowed and affirmed at the conclusion of the Orthodox liturgy: 'We have seen the true light.' This is not poetical license; it is liturgical truth.

3. THE WOUND OF KNOWLEDGE: THEOLOGY AS DARKNESS

No one has ever seen God. (John 1:18)

What we have seen with our eyes, this we declare.
(1 John 1:1–3)

AUTHORITY AND TRADITION

There is, with reference to Orthodox spirituality, perhaps no aspect more often misunderstood than that of authority and tradition. In the Orthodox Church, the authority of the early Fathers, of the communion of saints, reveals a virtual continuity and contiguity between tradition and Christ. There is, here, no stifling enslavement to tradition but rather a striking embodiment of tradition, whose authority lies more in living and less in professing or decreeing. So, then, fidelity to tradition becomes a creative attitude, revealed in the lives of holy men and women; it is a tradition that lives. To meet a person who embraces and embodies this tradition is to encounter a paragon of authenticity and of integrity. It is precisely the same authority that is articulated in conciliar definitions and theological treatises throughout the centuries.

The Church Fathers are, therefore, recognised in the Orthodox Church as the privileged witnesses to and the historical links with a culture and period otherwise so distant in time and perception from our world. In the spiritual development of the Orthodox, remembering these Fathers is more than an occasion to recall one's heritage and memory. It is an opportunity to rekindle a flame or re-present the past. It is a way of re-appropriating the sacred values and holy virtues of those who 'walked in the same way in which Christ walked' (1 John 2:6), of recognising that we constitute members of the same body of Christ (Eph. 5:30). One contemporary Orthodox theologian and monk eloquently describes the experience of approaching the early Fathers:

> I am reading St. Isaac the Syrian. I find something true, heroic, spiritual in him; something which transcends space and time. I feel that here, for the first time, is a voice that resonates in the deepest parts of my being, hitherto closed and unknown to me. Although he is so far removed from me in time and space, he has come right into the house of my soul. In a moment of quiet he has spoken to me, sat down beside me. Although I have read so many things, although I have met so many other people, and though today there are others living around me, no one else has been so discerning. To no one else have I opened the door of my soul in this way. Or to put it better, no one else has shown me into such a space, which is open and unlimited. And no one else has told me this unexpected and ineffable truth, namely that the whole of this inner world belongs to us. For the first time I feel a holy pride in our human – or better, our divine-human – nature, an amazement before it. The presence of a saint, separated from the world and from the stain of sin, has given me this divine blessing. He belongs to our human nature. I rejoice at this. I enjoy the benefits of his blessing. Being of the same nature as myself, he really transfuses the life-giving blood of his freedom into me. He shows me human personhood as it truly is. By his presence he tells me that we are together, and I feel that it is so. This is not something foreign to me. He is himself my most true self. He is an unblemished flower of our human nature.[1]

THE CHURCH OF THE FATHERS: THE AUTHORITY OF ANTIQUITY

When listening to some Christians today, one may easily receive the impression that God stopped speaking to the Church and to the world around two thousand years ago. According to their view there were certain golden ages in history when God was more freely and profusely revealed, after which God withdrew, leaving us 'in the dark' ages, so to speak. All that remained as points of light was the testimony of those who lived during these charismatic eras. In the Orthodox Church, however, there is a conviction that, while there was indeed a remarkable working of the Holy Spirit in the early years of Christianity, that charismatic immanence was but the beginning of a tradition, not the end of it. Rejecting the continual and continued presence of living saints in the Church is tantamount to denying the living presence of the Spirit of God within the Church. In a very real sense, then, it is the flames and not the ashes of the Church Fathers that are remembered.

Nevertheless, in the minds of many, sometimes even Orthodox themselves, the title 'Church Fathers' is restricted to the teachers of the *ancient* Church. They might include such classic representatives as Basil of Caesarea (d. 379), Gregory Nazianzus, the Theologian (d. *c.* 390), and John Chrysostom (d. 407). Moreover, it is normally assumed that the authority of the Fathers depends, at least partially, on antiquity, namely on their *historical* proximity to the early Church and to Christ, to the age of the Apostles and Martyrs. Few appreciate that this authority is in fact largely due to the quality of the patristic testimony, namely to their closeness to the *faith* – and not simply to the times – of the Apostles.

In the spiritual tradition and life of the Orthodox Church, there is certainly no sense of any such interruption from the 'primitive' Christian age. The overall structure of the liturgical cycle still follows the early patterns and cycles, while the Orthodox Church in general continues to follow the way of the

Fathers. Those who cannot accept this continuity either regret the backwardness of the Eastern Church or else retire into a conservative theology of repetition. What then assumes interest and importance are the frescoes and manuscripts, the syntax and concepts, the dress and behaviour of the time, and not the less conspicuous life of the Church Fathers and Mothers, or the writings that resulted from their spirituality.

No one can deny the theological brilliance of Church Fathers in the fourth and fifth centuries, but to denigrate the significance of later writers would result in a distorted theological vision. Maximus the Confessor (d. 662), Symeon the New Theologian (d. 1022) and Gregory Palamas (d. 1359) would be unthinkable and unintelligible without the Cappadocians; they are not merely 'appendices' to the earlier Fathers. Restrictive formulas such as 'the Church of the Seven Councils' and 'the Byzantine Church' (sometimes adopted by Orthodox scholars themselves) may prove exclusive if used without qualification, limiting the spiritual authority of the Church to certain favoured periods. The Church has by no means ceased to think and live creatively since the seventh Ecumenical Council (787).

THE AUTHENTICITY OF SPIRITUAL KNOWLEDGE

So the fullness of the Church cannot be interpreted statically; it must be articulated in dynamic terms. Similarly, the authority of the Church cannot be limited, whether to five or eight or more centuries, because it always contains the force and fire of Pentecost. Whether in the seclusion of the desert, in the community of a monastery or in the life of the world, the Church Fathers are themselves aware of no rupture or change in theology or spirituality. Thus the *Philokalia* of Nikodemus of Mount Athos (1749–1809) includes writings from the early age of St Antony of Egypt up until the Hesychasts of the fourteenth century, and its compiler, St Nikodemus, is himself considered a Church Father. All the saints are included, at least in theory, within the scope of the spiritual classics. Indeed, the age of the Fathers arguably continues up until the present day.

For a clearer appreciation of this open-ended scope of the spiritual tradition, the basic principle of Gregory the Theologian concerning theology is especially helpful. If we accept Gregory's axiomatic definition of theologians as being 'those tried and advanced in spiritual vision and, above all, those purified or, at least, undergoing purification',[2] then we must acknowledge that the high points of theology are not confined to one specific 'golden' age but rather pervade every age that happens to be blessed with those 'advanced in *theoria* . . . and purified'. By analogy, there is decay in the theological world and wisdom when such saints are wanting. It would be more appropriate to speak not of a golden age, but of a golden chain of spiritual continuity. In fact, it may be easier today to demonstrate the *historical* importance of, for example, the liturgy or monasticism, but what is much more important is to realise their ongoing vital influence in the *spiritual* life of the Church.

> Ecclesiastical Tradition is always being created; the process never stops; it is not only the past, but also the present . . . Tradition is not a sort of archaeology, which by its shadow connects the present with the past, nor a law. It is the fact that the life of the Church remains always identical with itself . . . Nothing is more false than the idea . . . of the Eastern Church as the Church of Tradition, a Church frozen into an immobility of ritualism and traditionalism. [3]

To claim, then, that there are no Fathers or Mothers today is to deny the living presence of the Holy Spirit within the Church. As Symeon the New Theologian wrote in the tenth century, it is heresy and a subversion of Scripture to claim that later generations are denied access to the Holy Spirit or cannot acquire the same vision of God enjoyed by the saints: 'One who makes this claim subverts all the divine Scriptures. Those who make these claims shut up the heaven that Christ opened for us, and cut off the way opened for us.'[4]

TRADITION AND TRADITIONALISM

The entire history of the Orthodox Church is marked by this keen sense of *continuity with the past*. In twentieth-century Istanbul (formerly Constantinople, and still the See of the Ecumenical Patriarch), the Patriarchate is known as 'Rum Patrikhanesi' (or the Roman Patriarchate), while the Greeks of the Polis (or capital 'city' of the Byzantine Empire) continue to call themselves 'Romaioi' or 'Romioi' (Romans). This phenomenon is not restricted to the Greeks; the Antiochene Christians likewise refer to themselves as 'Rhum'.

Behind these somewhat unexpected nomenclatures, there lies an historical fact of great significance. In the West, the Roman Empire collapsed under the pressure of barbarian invasions during the fifth century, and the medieval society that slowly emerged from the ruins, while having many links with the past and claiming still to be the 'Holy Roman Empire', fundamentally differed from the preceding. However, the East knew no such sudden break in the history of the Roman Empire. There, the Roman Empire survived for a thousand years longer. Despite profound religious, economic, political and social changes, and in spite of its gradual divergence from the classical Roman culture, its Hellenization, and its progressive decline in size and resources, the Byzantine Empire remained – at least until the fall of Constantinople in 1453 – essentially the same Roman Empire as that over which Augustus had ruled in the first century of the Christian era.

Moreover, and more importantly, the East maintained the same doctrine, liturgy, spirituality and theology as developed by the early Christian community. Anyone studying Byzantine history or theology must constantly bear this factor of continuity in mind. For while historians and other scholars may distinguish, for the sake of convenience, between the Roman and the Byzantine empires, there is actually no clear line of demarcation between the two; the Byzantine is to be seen rather as a continuation of the Roman Empire. This, at least, is how the Byzantines in the past and how the Orthodox of today have understood their identity.

The Byzantine East never experienced a 'Middle Ages' in the Western sense of the term. The approach to theology and the spiritual life in Byzantium always remained basically uniform, fundamentally Patristic, and the Byzantines continued to think and theologise in much the same fashion as the early Church Fathers. There was really nothing in the East that proved comparable to the Scholastic revolution or, later, to the cultural Renaissance and Western Reformation. Thus, for an Eastern Christian of the fourteenth century – the time of the monastic defender, Gregory Palamas, and the liturgical commentator, Nicholas Cabasilas – the centuries-old Fathers of the Church were members of the same world; they were regarded and even revered as spiritual Fathers and guides; in a vital sense, they were contemporaries.

THE ASCETICAL AND MYSTICAL DIMENSION

In the Orthodox theological world-view, then, it may not be appropriate to speak of doctrinal development as such. It may be more precise to refer to spiritual direction. The understanding is that we learn and become familiar with the principles of faith from particular individuals. The reality of the Christian experience and doctrine is not something picked up only in books. After all, even in discovering insights from written material, we are always in the context of learning from others. It is similar to the way in which we begin to speak, or indeed begin to pray. We learn from others.

People in earlier centuries – or rather throughout the centuries – visited a wise director in the desert of Egypt in order to 'ask for a word of salvation'. These words were collected and edited, but the heart of the experience remained the word of a holy elder spoken to a specific person in a specific historical and cultural setting. The living voice of those who through prayer, self-discipline and love have come to know the heart of the faith, has a certain immediacy and directness, and incarnates the fundamental experience of encounter with the living God. Such elders do not seek to replace God but rather to initiate others into the mystery of God. Spiritual direction comprises the subject of particular attention in Chapter 8. However, the relationship between *doctor* and *doctrine* is important to recognise here.

This relationship between doctors and doctrines by no means implies that a sinful person cannot read theology or live spiritually. Rather, in the Orthodox way, it means that a person who does not live according to Christ, yet who justifies himself or herself as doing so, will in fact create a theology that is according to his or her own measure and to his or her own taste, but not necessarily Orthodox. Knowledge is said to be given by God to the person who knows himself or herself to be fallible. Such a conviction is evident, for example, in the writings of the fourth-century Evagrius of Pontus and of the seventh-century Isaac the Syrian: 'Blessed are you when you know your weakness. For this knowledge becomes for you the foundation and source of all good things.'[5]

All this adds a dimension to Orthodox theology, which renders it both transcendent and immanent.[6] The gnostic dimension lies in its very surmounting of thought and surpassing of knowledge (Phil. 4:7). In classical terminology, this state is called 'ignorance' or 'silence'. It is the ignorance that is beyond all concepts, and the silence that is above all words. It is an opening up to a reality beyond, an opening out to a thought which does not seize but which finds itself seized (Gal. 4:9). This silence is the language of the world to come. Truth is profoundly mystical, never merely intellectual. It is a reality that ultimately cannot be told. It is a knowledge that is translated into love and life. In the words of Vladimir Lossky (1903–58):

> Knowledge of God writes itself into a personal relationship expressed in terms of reciprocity: reciprocity with

the object of theology (which, in reality, is a subject), reciprocity also with those to whom the theological word is addressed. At its best, it is communion: I know as I am known.[7]

Indeed, truth is a reality that already *is not* when *it is* described as what *it is*. Theology and the spiritual life simply attempt to express – or at least to suggest – the ineffable, the inexpressible. They are the language of silence translated as poetry, as liturgy, as doxology and as life. This is exactly why the *apophatic* (or negative) way is essential to Orthodox theology and spirituality. The philosophical technique of negation – known as apophaticism – is not a purely intellectual exercise but essentially a means of prostration before the living, personal God, who is radically unobjectifiable and ungraspable as personal and life-affirming. The unknowable God can be known only in communion and participation. The basis is, of course, scriptural: 'No one has ever seen God. It is only the Son of God, who is in the bosom of the Father, who has made God known to us' (John 1:18). This is the foundation of a language that through *apophasis* (or negation) opens up to the silence of *theosis* (or deification). It is the recognition that every method and means falls short of mystical truth, approaching truth only when it acknowledges its inability and incapacity to do so.

This leads us to one of the most distinctive marks of Orthodox theology, namely its 'existential' character. Theology is a potent and transforming message. The ultimate reference is always to the vision of faith, and separated from the life in Christ theology carries no conviction and is hardly convincing. In the seventh century, John Climacus underlined the need for direct, personal experience in anyone who claims to have some spiritual authority:

> A genuine teacher is one who has received from God the tablet of spiritual knowledge, inscribed by the divine finger, that is, by the inward working of illumination, and who has no need of other books. It is as unseemly for

teachers to give instruction from notes taken from other people's writings, as it is for painters to take inspiration from others' compositions.[8]

In the Orthodox tradition, doctrines are merely signposts (otherwise known as 'icons') in our journey towards God, pointers to (and never propositions about) the divine reality. This is why we like to refer to doctrine as being symbolical, as constituting a symbol of the word of God. Doctrine is a living *testimony* – in thought, word and experience – of what has been heard, seen and touched (1 John 1:1). It is the *tested* evidence of what has been contemplated in faith and experienced in love. This testimony may also be expressed in concepts and in definitions, albeit always inadequately.

Nevertheless, as a 'logical icon' of the living God, doctrine is the doxological expression of a truth received, expressed, celebrated and confessed in abundant fullness. Thus, in the minds and hearts of Orthodox believers, the search for doctrinal truth is also a search for doctrinal terminology. Doctrinal controversies, whether in the past or present, are often disputes over terms and words, precisely because these are never insignificant, even while insufficient. The words one adopts shape the values one assumes. The aim is always to develop a language that discerns mystery without dispelling it, to discover a method that appreciates mystery without either 'solving' or dissolving it:

> To say that the supreme Truth is beyond all formal expressions of itself accessible to the human intelligence is not to say that such expressions have no validity. On the contrary, they are an essential and indispensable part of any religion, for the simple reason that 'fallen' imperfect man is incapable of distinguishing for himself good from evil, truth from error, light from darkness. A formulation of the Truth, a doctrinal formulation, is valid, not because it contains the whole Truth in itself, for this is impossible, but because it provides, for those capable of

receiving it, a mental form through which a ray of this Truth is communicated.

In other words, doctrinal formulations have a double aspect. On the one hand, they 'reveal' the Truth in terms accessible to the human intelligence, and to this extent have an affirmative, or *kataphatic*, aspect, serving both as supports for man in his spiritual realization, and as defenses against such misconceptions of things as the human intelligence may be tempted to make; and, on the other hand, they are not the Truth itself, but merely its expression in human terms, and in this respect they have a negative, or *apophatic*, aspect.[9]

KNOWING THE UNKNOWABLE

Any lack of concern, however, for intellectualisation or systematisation does not imply a lack of efficiency in producing sound theology. Furthermore, in the Orthodox way, theology is never considered to be a monopoly of the professional academic or of the official hierarchy. Indeed, separated from the Church and the world, theology merely proves to be a sterile study of doctrinal formulations, rather than a deifying vision of deep conviction and commitment. The fact is that there is no external, juridically defined, criterion of truth, that orthodoxy is a common responsibility.

In an untheological world such as ours, it is difficult to imagine the degree to which religion once pervaded the entire spectrum of Eastern Christian life. It is sufficient to recall the words of Gregory of Nyssa, describing the unending theological discussions at the time of the Second Ecumenical Council (Constantinople, 381):

> The whole city is full of it, the squares, the market places, the cross-roads, the alley-ways; old-clothesmen, money changers, food sellers – they are all busy arguing. If you ask someone to give you change, they philosophize about the Begotten; if you inquire about the price of bread, you are told by way of reply that the Father is greater and the

Son inferior; if you ask whether your bath is ready, the attendant answers that the Son was made out of nothing.[10]

THEOLOGY POSITIVE AND NEGATIVE

As already observed, Orthodox theology and life cannot be properly understood without an appreciation of the negative or apophatic dimension. The concept of apophaticism is usually associated with the writings of Dionysius the Areopagite (end of the fifth century), although this form of theology is not an innovation of Dionysius. Already in Scripture there are allusions to the importance of darkness or *apophasis*, while it is fully developed as early as the fourth century with the Cappadocians, particularly in their treatises against Eunomius who claimed that the human intellect could know the very essence of God. Gregory of Nyssa expressed this in the following way:

> The true knowledge and vision of God consists in this: in seeing that God is invisible, because what we see lies beyond all knowledge, being wholly separated by the darkness of incomprehensibility . . . What is the significance of the fact that Moses went right into the darkness and saw God there? At first sight, the account of this vision of God seems to contradict the earlier one. For, whereas on that occasion the divine was seen in light, this time the divine is seen in darkness. But we should not regard this as involving any inconsistency at the level of the mystical meaning which concerns us. Through it the Word is teaching us that, in its initial stages, religious knowledge comes to us as illumination . . . The closer one approaches the vision of God, the more one recognizes the invisible character of the divine nature.[11]

Orthodox theology affirms the absolute transcendence of God, while at the same time underlining divine immanence. The ascent of the human intellect towards God may be described as a creative-negation, a kind of positive-negativity; it is a process of elimination resembling the spiritual *katharsis* – a discarding of all forms of impurity or idolatry. The radical inaccessibility of God is not simply due to the fallen or sinful nature of humanity, but rather to the ontological gap between created and Creator. The uncreated Creator is inaccessible, incomprehensible and invisible to both human and celestial creatures.

Thus, we can never speak of God in the same manner that we do about human beings or the material world. 'God cannot be grasped by the mind,' wrote Evagrius of Pontus in the fourth century; 'if He could, then He would not be God.'[12] In the words of Gregory Palamas, the eminent fourteenth-century exponent of the apophatic way: 'If God is described as nature, then everything else is not nature. If that which is not God can be spoken of as nature, then God is not nature; and likewise God does not even exist if that which is not God is said to exist.'[13]

The impact that this kind of theology, emphasising as it does the distance between God and world, has on attitudes towards the natural environment is perhaps uncertain. Yet the apophatic approach should be understood more in the sense of 'God-talk' than of 'world-talk'. All religions adopt a fundamentally negative approach with respect to God, inasmuch as they are aware of God's awesome and divine transcendence. And the *via negativa* is also characteristic of Scholastic thought. Yet in Orthodox theology, apophaticism is not simply an intellectual method of approaching the mystery of God. It is not considered a better, more effective, way of knowing God. Byzantine theologians repeatedly refer to the authority of Basil the Great in this regard:

> The divine energies are manifold, but the essence is simple. As for us, we say that we know our God through his energies, whereas we never presume to approach his essence. The energies of God come down to us, while his essence remains inaccessible.[14]

In fact, this critical distinction between divine essence and divine energies is perhaps what also holds together a more balanced and inclusive cosmology. The conviction is that divine truth is never exhausted by the human intellect, even while it is expressed in love to the whole of creation.

An awareness of the radical transcendence of God leads to a positive and personal encounter with the One who is Unknown, to a knowledge that is beyond all knowledge, and ultimately to divine 'ignorance'. Theology, then, transcends all formulation and definition, being identified rather with a personal and loving relationship with God in the communion of prayer.[15]

God is not a rational problem requiring solution; rather, God is the lover of humanity and the world, granting communion and transfiguration. In such a communion and transfiguration, the desire is always insatiable and unending; it is the love of the bride in the Song of Songs, who stretches out her hands towards him that cannot be grasped, who reaches for him that cannot be attained. Thus, apophatic theology corresponds to mystical union with God, whose essence at all times remains inaccessible.

> The apophatic attitude gave to the Fathers of the Church that freedom and liberality with which they employed philosophical terms without running the risk of being misunderstood or of falling into a 'theology of concepts' . . . The apophatic way does not lead to an absence, to an utter emptiness; for the unknowable God of the Christian is not the impersonal God of the philosophers. It is to the Holy Trinity 'superessential, more than divine, and more than good' . . . that the author of the *Mystical Theology* commends himself in entering upon the way, which is to bring him to a presence and fullness, which are without measure.[16]

By the same token, the silence of *apophasis* can never be reduced to a mere cessation of speech. It is a positive and creative phenomenon, just as love and life itself are. It is no pause or interval between sounds, just as apophaticism does not simply denote agnosticism. Silence does not imply absence but quality and depth. For Abba Isaac the Syrian, 'revelation itself is silence of intellect'.[17] After all, in the words of his contemporary Maximus the Confessor, the source of all knowledge lies in 'knowing in supreme ignorance the supremely Unknowable'.[18]

4. TEARS AND BROKENNESS: THE WAY OF IMPERFECTION AND SPONTANEITY

And so I came to this true land of mourners.
(John Climacus)

There is no other way than tears. (Abba Poemen; Symeon the New Theologian)

One of the more tangible and 'natural' ways of expressing the darkness within, at least according to the classical texts of Orthodox spirituality, is the shedding of tears. The gift of tears is 'native' to Christianity and played a dominant role in ascetical and mystical expressions. It may be traced from the New Testament, through the early desert tradition, to John Climacus who added refreshing and remarkable dimensions, and then to later centuries, with Symeon the New Theologian, who had certainly read the *Ladder*, standing out as perhaps the greatest witness.

The Eastern Church has in fact served as a cradle for this treasure given to Christianity by Jesus, who 'blessed those who mourn' (Matt. 5:4).[1] While not unknown in the Western spiritual tradition, especially in writers such as John Cassian – who, nonetheless, learned about the 'deep waters of the heart' while living with the early desert fathers of Egypt – tears were accorded priority in the East, perhaps on account of the emphasis on the heart as a vessel of the Holy Spirit. This chapter explores the phenomenon of tears in three classics of spirituality: (i) the desert fathers and mothers, who are the source of the two following great thinkers; (ii) John Climacus, the seventh-century hermit and abbot of Mount Sinai, and author of *The Ladder of Divine Ascent*; and (iii) Symeon the New Theologian, the most beloved and enthusiastic mystic of tenth-century Byzantium.

THE WAY OF THE DESERT: SPRINGS OF LIVING WATER

Tears are clearly a prized virtue in the desert tradition, symbolical of survival through the dryness of the desert. They are a silent way of learning and loving. The entire flight to the desert may be summarised in the priority and practice of weeping. Tears are a way of surrendering, of dying, although always in the context and in the hope of new life and resurrection. They are a way of embracing darkness in order to receive light.

> Abba Alonius said: 'If I had not destroyed myself completely, I would not have been able to rebuild and reshape myself again.'[2]

Abba Alonius' words may sound very harsh. Yet, it may be that by surrendering life we can rediscover ourselves. In struggling against what we are not, we are in fact seeking to discern what we truly are and to know ourselves. The reality is that we tend to forget who and what we are. Not that we may be tempted to imagine that we are more than we actually are; unfortunately, the reality is that we tolerate being *less than we are called to be*. Pride is not the ultimate sin; forgetfulness of our origin and destiny is, in fact, the ultimate tragedy.

No wonder, then, that the wisdom of the desert emphasised remembrance of death; it was another dimension to remembrance of God. The desert fathers and mothers embraced their mortality; they were comfortable with death. They recognised death as another way of connecting to themselves, to their neighbour and to God. So often, we endeavour to cheat death; we instinctively try to avoid or escape death. We do not want to face change, or pain, or passion, or death. And so, we search for ways to step away from death – financially, technologically, medically, emotionally.

Yet, the desert fathers and mothers advise us to stay silent and to stay put! They counsel us to shut the door and simply to sit in the cell! We are simply to wait, even as – indeed, *especially* when – we experience moments of panic, of power-lessness, of helplessness, of terror, of death. That is what they did. After all, where do you go beyond the desert? Where else do you go when you have climbed a thirty-foot pole, as the stylites of Syria did? Where can you go when, like Antony, you have moved from the outer desert to the inner desert of Egypt? You just sit; you just stay; you just wait. Then, when you arrive at the end of your individual resources, an infinite and eternal source can open up. Not that divine grace is absent before-hand; it is simply unnoticed while we yet depend on ourselves. So tears are the only way into the heart.

> Abba Poemen said: 'Weeping is the way that the Scriptures and the Fathers give us, when they say: "Weep!" Truly, there is no other way than this.' He also said: 'It is impossible not to weep, either voluntarily or when compelled through suffering.'[3]

The desert elders embrace human shortcoming and failure as the ultimate opportunity for divine grace and strength, which can only be 'perfected in weakness' (2 Cor. 12:9). This is precisely the framework within which they understand the role of tears. Early on, it seems, we lose that innate ability to grieve; and so we must learn, gradually and painfully, to acquire it again.

> Abba Poemen also said: 'Truly, there is no other way than this!'[4]

For the desert fathers and mothers, there is no stage beyond this knowledge of imperfection. Perfection is for God, not for us; imperfection is ours to acknowledge and to know, not to forego or forget. In the desert, the gospel injunction to 'be perfect, as your heavenly Father is perfect' (Matt. 5:48) becomes a vision of realism. It does not remain some vague dream or romanticism. For these elders, life is a perpetual standing beneath the cross, an unceasing weeping. And the source, the object of these tears is the light of the resurrection that shines beyond the cross, transforming sorrow into joy:

> Abba Joseph related that Abba Isaac said: 'I was sitting with Abba Poemen one day, and I saw him in ecstasy. And, as I was on terms of great freedom of speech with him, I begged him saying: "Tell me where you were." He said: "My thought was with Saint Mary, the Mother of God, as she wept by the cross of the Savior. I wish I could always weep like that."'[5]

As we shall see below, what is far more important and far more insightful than learning to live is learning to die.

TEARS IN ST JOHN CLIMACUS: A SPIRITUALITY OF IMPERFECTION

Tears are a way of knowing ourselves; we weep because we have lost our paradisial identity, or else because we are homesick for a 'lost paradise'. There is, here, an intense element of nostalgia and desire. For John Climacus, the seventh-century abbot of the monastery on Mount Sinai (*c.* 579–*c.* 649), even a single day passed without tears of repentance is a day wasted.[6] Such repentance is not a self-generating act or condition: it is a passing over – a *pascha* or Passover – from death to life and a continual renewal of that life. It consists of a reversal of what has become the normal pattern of development, the movement from life to death. It is a new life or 'resurrection'. It is, as John says, 'a contract with God for a second life' (5.2; *PG* 88:764).

Tears and Baptism

Tears wash away sins 'both seen and perceived' (7.33; *PG* 88:808); they 'resemble a bath'. John plays with the verbs *piptein* (to fall) and *niptein* (to wash). Such statements have an unmistakable baptismal connotation. Indeed, in step seven, John makes what he admits is a bold assertion: 'Greater than baptism itself is the fountain of tears after baptism, though it is somewhat daring to say so' (7.8; *PG* 88:804). While John speaks in similar fashion elsewhere (5.5; *PG* 88:764 and 26.25; *PG* 88:1021), there is no suggestion of substituting tears for the sacrament of baptism. John is perfectly aware of the unique status of baptism, even in the above passage, where he states – in deliberately paradoxical fashion – that on the one hand tears may be 'greater' than baptism, while on the other hand tears follow 'after' baptism.

Tears never replace but rather renew baptism; they do not grant divine grace but bring to our awareness a grace already bestowed in baptism. The force of tears is precisely a rejuvenating one, a continuation or rejuvenation of baptism's cleansing function, with no implication of any duplication of baptism's sacramental power. The supremacy or efficacy of the sacrament is never in question. Instead, there is an affirmation of the need for conscious receptivity of and continual response to baptismal grace.[7] Tears mark the tension and transition between being and becoming.

Tears as Charisma

The connection, however, between baptism and tears implies that tears are not pursued by our own human effort but occur spontaneously or gratuitously. Spiritual tears flow without contraction of facial muscles; they are a consequence of divine grace: 'The Lord has come uninvited, giving us the sponge of God-loving sorrow and the cool water of devout tears' (7.27; *PG* 88:805). This phenomenon is well illustrated by the thirteenth-century French tale about 'Le chevalier au Barizel', once ordered to fill a barrel with water. He travels all over the world to achieve this, yet the water always passes through the barrel. Seeing that his efforts achieve nothing, he weeps; and that one teardrop is sufficient to fill the barrel.

As a gift, tears testify to a divine visitation. Moreover, this is preceded by an earlier visitation from the Uninvited Guest, who arrives but later leaves us to mourn the divine absence. To wait is to weep; to weep is to be humble. Waiting is the surest way of attaining the divine gift. And patience is critical because the oncoming of tears is gradual: literally, drop by drop (8.1; *PG* 88:828).[8] God gives and God takes: indeed, the giving, the taking and the withholding are all part of the way of tears. Deprivation, too, may be a token of restitution. Tears symbolise the fullness of life, with all of its sorrows and joys. I weep; therefore, I am! Tears of joy come at the end – not at the beginning – of a long and painful inner struggle.

Overture of Joy

John's most original contribution to the theology of tears lies in his identification of sorrow with joy. The technical terms he adopts for the state of joyful sorrow – *charopoion penthos* and *charmolype* – are found for the first time in his writings, while the seventh chapter, which is devoted to this subject, has proved the most influential part of the *Ladder*. For John, the bitterness of tears is sweetened through repentance; tears of fear blossom into tears of love. Tears are at once the foretaste of death and the foretaste of resurrection.

Herein lies the positive or 'beautiful' dimension of mourning; Climacus speaks of 'the beauty of mourning'. Humanity has lost the balance between joy and sorrow found in 'the beauty of mourning'. The concept marks Climacus' dialectical approach: repentance is a balance of perdition and resurrection, of death and life, of despair and hope (5.2; *PG* 88:764 and 5.5; *PG* 88:776).

Moreover, 'the loftiness of lowliness' (5.9; *PG* 88:777) reflects the simultaneous experience of Gethsemane and Tabor, of Holy Friday and Easter Sunday commingled and condensed: 'dying, and behold living . . . sorrowful, yet always rejoicing' (2 Cor. 6:9–10). John describes this as being 'filled with joy and sorrow – joy at seeing the beloved, and sorrow at being deprived for so long of that fair beauty' (7.57; *PG* 88:813). With this teaching,

John condenses the whole evangelical and patristic teaching. Other writers may allude to joyful sorrow, but John explicitly develops the concept for the first time. The 'miraculous' transformation from 'painful' to 'painless tears' overwhelms John himself: 'I am amazed at how what is called mourning and grief contains joy and gladness interwoven within it, like honey in a comb' (7.50; *PG* 88:812).

There is an underlying optimism in John's teaching about tears. Human nature was created for joy and not for sorrow, for laughter and not for tears: 'God does not desire that we mourn with sorrowful heart, but rather that we rejoice with spiritual laughter' (7.45; *PG* 88:809). As an expression of love, spiritual joy excludes darkness: 'Remove sin, and the tear of sorrow is superfluous. What is the use of a bandage when there is no wound?' (7.46; *PG* 88:809). This may appear to be at variance with other statements on tears, but it is consistent with John's conception of spiritual joy. There is 'a time to weep and a time to laugh' (Eccles. 3:4) (26.59; *PG* 88:1032 and 7.67; *PG* 88:816), and our joy is complete only when we have arrived home. There is joy in arriving and joy in being on the way (7.46; *PG* 88:809). Joy (*chara*) and grace (*charis*) share a common root and significance – etymologically, theologically and spiritually.

The Silent Way Within

Now, at first glance, the total effect of the *Ladder* gives a negative impression. Sixteen out of the thirty steps deal with vices to be avoided and, of the remaining fourteen, some are again seemingly negative: repentance, sorrow and dispassion. Nevertheless, this initial impression could be misleading, because the sixteen steps dealing with the vices deal at the same time with the corresponding virtues and are much shorter than the other fourteen, which themselves are also not as negative as they may at first appear.

Yet the balance between negativity and positivity goes much deeper than such a superficial observation. John is not afraid of negative elements or the darker dimensions of the heart. He does not regard these merely as temporary stages, but recognises in them the very transcendence of human failure and finality. Like the desert fathers and mothers, John also appreciates human sin and failure as the ultimate opportunity for divine grace and strength, which can only be 'perfected in weakness' (2 Cor. 12:9).

Tears are unfortunately often perceived as a negative aspect of the spiritual life. Few comprehend that tears of brokenness, as symbols of imperfection, are in fact the *sole* way of spiritual progress. John does not write about deification; he simply records the long journey of the way, the gradual stages, the painful steps towards this sublime goal. He knows that this alone lies within our grasp and realism. He is convinced that one silent tear will advance us more in the spiritual way than any number of louder ascetic feats or more visible virtuous achievements.

The silence of tears is a way of interiority, a way of exploring the inaccessible cellars of the heart. Through sorrow, we learn by suffering and undergoing, not just by understanding. The connection between tears and silence is important. Words are a way of affirming our existence and of justifying our actions and emotions. Yet silence, which can almost feel like death, is a way of surrendering all self-justification. Through tears, we give up our infantile images of God and give in to the living image of God. We confess our personal powerlessness and profess divine powerfulness. Tears confirm our readiness to allow our life to fall apart in the dark night of the soul, and our willingness to assume new life in the resurrection of the dead.

When we admit our hopelessness and desperation and recognise that we have 'hit rock bottom' in our relationships with people and with God, we also discover the compassion of a God who voluntarily assumed the vulnerability of crucifixion. One would not seek divine healing unless one had to in order to survive, until one admitted there was no other way out of the impasse. Our hearts are the dwelling-places of God, but all of

them are made of glass. Tears signify this fragility, wounded-
ness and brokenness.

God finds and enters the open wound – the broken window,
that teardrop – of our heart, bringing healing to the soul and
the world, not in order simply to comfort but rather to identify
with us in an act of infinite and healing compassion. God
understands, having undergone the vulnerability of assuming
child-likeness and death on a cross. Such vulnerability is the
only way towards holiness. The more profound our personal
misery, the more abundant God's eternal mercy; the deeper
the abyss of human corruption, the greater the grace of heavenly compassion; the more involved our exposure to the way
of the cross, the more intense our experience of the light of
resurrection.

John reveals extraordinarily subtle insight into 'the mysterious land of tears'. His teaching on tears is a theology of
depth, revealing the fragility of life and unveiling a spirituality of imperfection. For John, like for the inhabitants of the
early Egyptian desert, life is a continual balance of tensions. It
is the way through the abyss of the cross to the boundless light
of the resurrection.

TEARS IN SYMEON THE NEW THEOLOGIAN: A
SPIRITUALITY OF SPONTANEITY

Symeon the New Theologian (949–1022) stands out as the
greatest witness and most articulate spokesman of the way of
tears.[9] Symeon first learned about tears from the *Ladder*,
which he read before embracing the monastic life. However, his
understanding of tears was derived directly from his own
spiritual master, Symeon the Studite (also known as the
'pious'), and was transmitted faithfully to his own spiritual
disciple, Nicetas Stethatos. It is a theology experienced
through a living tradition of tears and not simply learned
through books. Indeed, this personal and powerful experience
of the way of tears marks the very beginning of Symeon's own
spiritual and mystical journey, when – after his vision of divine

light as a young man called George – Symeon tells us that he 'was flooded with tears, weeping from his heart, while his tears were accompanied by sweetness'.[10]

The Silence of Tears

It is, then, more important to shed tears than to define them, to undergo them rather than merely to understand them. Symeon himself struggles to articulate what is essentially an inexpressible reality, an ecstatic experience. How exactly can anyone describe the effect of divine grace, of being touched by God? How can anyone adequately communicate the impact of the wound of divine love, of the soul being smitten – Symeon prefers the term 'bitten' – by God's love?

> When tears purify your eyes and you see Him whom no person has ever seen; when your soul is bitten by His love and you compose a song mingled with tears, please remember me. For, then, you have attained to union with God and to boldness with Him.[11]

As noted, tears make their appearance when words are either rendered insufficient or else exhausted. They leave behind conventional human language. Or, more accurately, tears transform and consecrate words; they create a new language, another way of communication. Perhaps 'song' and 'boldness' are the only appropriate ways of expressing the way of tears. Perhaps there is insufficient song and poetry in our theology and church life. Perhaps there is too little boldness and confidence in our personal and social life. Tears provide a sense of faithfulness in our relationship with God and one another. They reveal a dimension of interiority and intensity. They are a way of spontaneity and authenticity. More than merely reversing an emphasis on rationalism or complementing the rigidity of intellectualism, tears symbolise wholeness and integrity. More than simply permitting any form of sentimentalism or questioning the mistrust of emotionalism, tears affirm identity and vividness. Tears are silent; yet they are filled with sound and song. They are our true voice, our mother tongue.

The Essence of Tears

For Symeon, tears are at the same time a gift and a way, both an endowment and an effort. They are the fire of God's presence that warms the heart and the water of the ascetic's prayer that extinguishes sins.[12] When we weep, we stop; tears are an opportunity to slow down and to stop, to be silent and simply to be. They are a tangible manifestation – or incarnation – of our conscious contact with God. You cannot move on until and unless you first stop; you cannot receive the Spirit until and unless you first surrender your self; you cannot find your soul if you do not first lose it (Matt. 10:39). In what we lose and find, we discover the mystery; our tear-filled eyes are opened to the face of God. Indeed, Symeon compares tears to water and rain, which bring a garden to fruition: without the givenness of tears (the gift of divine *charis*) as well as the effort to irrigate (the struggle of human *ascesis*), flowers will not blossom and vegetables will not mature.[13]

Yet, tears are by no means an expression of mere passivity, of passively or patiently awaiting God's action; they are an active manifestation of the soul's willingness to progress – or, in fact, to undergo the process of return.[14] Tears are the recognition that we are 'living, and partly living' (T. S. Eliot, *Murder in the Cathedral*) and an expression of our desire to 'have life, and life in abundance' (John 10:10). Silently probing the waters of the heart is the beginning of life in the Spirit. Perhaps this is why there is a close connection between tears and baptism. Tears are not a sentimental reaction, but a sincere regeneration, a moment of resurrection. Ultimately, tears are a way of seeing more clearly, of cleansing the eyes and sharpening the vision.[15]

Tears may appear to be expressed outwardly, but in fact they are produced from within and aim precisely at turning us inward.

Things are different. For, God does not show any external favor; nor does He look only to the outward correction of our conduct or listen to our audible cries. God considers a broken and contrite heart.[16]

Tears are not at all about 'doing' but always about 'being'. The aim of the spiritual life, for Symeon, is to become 'all Christ', a child of God, a direct heir of the living God. God does not have grandchildren; God only begets: 'I, too, become god unconsciously; He begets me ineffably, spiritually. What an amazing event!'[17] Tears are a direct result of 'travailing in childbirth until Christ is formed inside us' (Gal. 4:19):

Just as a woman, who is pregnant, knows that a child is moving inside her womb; and she cannot be oblivious to its presence; so also does the one in whom Christ is being formed. Such a person understands Christ's movings, also known as His illuminations.[18]

Like John Climacus, Symeon also speaks of a visitation from God. We await the Divine Visitor.[19] Where tears abound, the grace of God also flourishes. Such a divine visitation or illumination, where new light breaks into the heart, implies a particular knowledge. Through tears, we receive the light of Christ within; we are en-lightened; through tears, we receive the life of the Spirit within; we are in-spired.

Tears enable the heart to recognise both the presence and the absence of God. We can only weep for whom or what we actually know, and not merely imagine. This knowledge is the sole criterion of our spiritual progress. Virtue and sin are measured solely by the degree of this knowledge, not by any accumulated merits or faults. When the knowledge of God – whether of his presence or even his absence – assumes greater significance than any particular virtues or vices, then the outer person grows attuned to the inner person. Then, the bitter and dark roots of the heart are embraced as part and parcel of the sweet and apparent flowers on the surface. Then, one knows that 'the kingdom of God lies within' (Luke 17:21). Then, tears

– like heaven itself – flow from within as the surprise of new life, marking the dawn also of new light.

Nothing external can ever measure, predict or exhaust us. We are a work of beauty in progress, forever the same and yet ever developing and changing. This is why we can gain – or lose – paradise at any given moment. More perhaps than any other writer of the early Church, Symeon is well aware of this truth: that the lost can be found, the sick healed, the dead brought to life. Changes are real; in the history of spirituality, they are called conversions. A loss can become a triumph in seed, a curse can be a blessing in disguise, a 'people in darkness can see the great light; and for those who have sat in the region and the shadow of death, light has dawned' (Matt. 4:16).

When the heart is crushed under 'the very light and sweet stone of holy humility' in order to allow the liquid flow, then:

> The soul is watered with floods of tears, making the living water to spring up, curing the wounds caused by one's sins, washing the pus and ulcers from the soul … Then, as a result of this, even snow appears less brilliant, and that person is revealed to be whole.[20]

Such vulnerability and openness, the result of being crushed ever so lightly and sweetly by God – or by life – inevitably renders the heart more spontaneous and responsive. It also seals the heart with the distinctive mark of holiness. Orthodox theology emphasises the importance and centrality of deification or *theosis*. *Theosis* is no less, and no more, than falling down and getting back up, starting anew. If our eyes enjoy the vision of God (the mystery of becoming God), then it is because our tears can express the beauty of humanity (the mystery of being human). Tears are the ultimate and most intimate companions of deification, our sure escape route from death to life:

> Through the constant watering and cooling of tears, the flame of divine desire burns all the more brightly within us, producing ever more copious tears, washing us by

their flow and causing us to shine with greater radiance. Then, when we are completely enflamed and entirely enlightened, we become as light; and the words of the Divine John are fulfilled: 'God is united with gods and is known by them.'[21]

5. A SILENT TRADITION: EARLY MONASTICISM AND CONTEMPORARY EXPRESSIONS

Silence is a mystery of the world to come. (Abba Isaac the Syrian)

Athos, mountain of silence! (Philip Sherrard)

There is a phrase in the alphabetical collection of the fifth-century *Sayings of the Desert Fathers* with which I am able to identify:

> One day Macarius the Egyptian went from Scetis to the mountain of Nitria for the offering of Abba Pambo. The old man said to him: 'Father, say a word to the brethren.' He said: 'I have not yet become a monk myself, but *I have seen monks*.'[1]

I am not a monk, but I have been privileged to study classical literature of the early desert and to encounter genuine representatives of the mountain of silence. It is from this experience that I write of the tradition of silence.

THE THREE MONASTIC WAYS

According to the traditional account, monasticism began in Egypt on Sunday morning, probably in our equivalent of the third week of Great Lent, in the year 270 or 271. The Gospel of the day included the words: 'If you want to be perfect, go, sell what you possess and give to the poor, and you will have treasure in heaven; and come, follow me' (Matt. 19:21). In the congregation, there was a young man called Antony. Upon hearing these words, Antony decided to enter the uninhabited desert. He sought not merely poverty but complete solitude. Antony's step was little noticed outside (perhaps even inside) his village at the time, but when he died, at the ripe old age of 106, his biographer Athanasius said that his reputation spread all over the world. 'The desert had become a city.'[2]

Of course it did not begin exactly like that. The genuine historical origins of Christian monasticism are veiled in mystery. We need first of all to recall non-Christian monastic movements, since the phenomenon is not distinctively Christian, answering as it does to a deep, perhaps universal, human instinct. Second, contemporary research shows that Syriac monasticism is at least as ancient as the Egyptian and in fact developed there quite independently. However, in Syria and elsewhere, there is no *one* person, at least not like Antony – at least not as Athanasius spoke and wrote of Antony.

Still, the myth that it all began in Egypt with Antony and the other monks of that desert is true to some extent inasmuch as it is to them that succeeding generations of monastics always look back for inspiration. Antony may not be the founder, but he is clearly the father of monasticism. Orthodox monks and nuns of today would certainly feel part of his tradition.

By the mid-fourth century, Egypt was a land of monastic settlements, with three distinctive types of monastic life emerging. There is, first, the *eremitical* form, where the model is Antony himself. Second, there is the *cenobitic* form (or communal style); here, the founder and model is Pachomius. Finally, there is the *semi-eremitic/semi-cenobitic* type, centred in Nitria and Scetis; the founder of this third way is Abba Amoun.[3] The pre-eminence of Eastern monasticism moved to Asia Minor in the late fourth century, to Palestine in the fifth and sixth, to Sinai in the seventh and eighth, and to Athos from the ninth and tenth centuries.

These three ways survive to this day on Mount Athos, a peninsula of Northern Greece and a remarkable example of continuity in Eastern monasticism. There is the eremitic region, where a desolate piece of land invites a life of solitude, practised in the ninth century by Peter the Athonite. This area is still known as the *eremos* on Mount Athos – undesertlike in many ways, yet also isolated by its cliffs. There is also the region known as the *scete* or *lavra* – a collection of hermitages, more or less widely scattered and normally established around the common focus of one hermit, who has retreated there and subsequently attracted a number of disciples. Here, we have the example on Athos of Euthymius the Younger (b. 823), who lived for three years in a cave and gathered around himself a group of disciples. Finally, there is the stricter rule of the monastery proper, with fixed regulations and definite buildings, under the direction of an abbot. The earliest example of this form on Athos is the monastery of Athanasius the Athonite (d. 997). Today, there are twenty such communities on the Mountain, dating from 963 to the early part of the fifteenth century. The centre of prayer for over a thousand years, it has earned the epithet 'holy', now an intrinsic part of its name: *Agion Oros*, or 'Holy Mountain'.

All the monasteries share a rich heritage. Imperial seals and gifts are proudly exhibited; the buildings bear the scars of their long, turbulent past: Crusaders, Saracens, Franks and Catalans have left their mark. Above all, however, these communities share an added treasure. The extraordinary geographical condition and position of Athos – its craggy isolation, as well as its proximity to the shores of Greece and Asia Minor – traditionally rendered it suitable to the solitary life. The lack of natural harbours, the plummeting southern cliffs, the alarming suddenness of its storms – all contribute to seclusion and immunity. Athos is a natural peninsula of sacred silence.

The entire scenery of the mountain underlines the essence of the silence sought by its inhabitants: they travel there, withdrawing from society in order to overcome the divisions and tensions within, and so become 'simple' (cf. Matt. 6:22) – which may well have been one of the original meanings of the

Greek word for 'monk' (*monachos*). This simple-ness or single-ness reveals another dimension of monastic celibacy: one remains single in order to be unified. And silence is a way to this end.

TWO LEVELS OF SILENCE

One of the key texts for the appreciation of silence is *The Ladder of Divine Ascent*, written by the seventh-century abbot of the Sinaite monastery of Saint Catherine, John Climacus. The *Ladder* has an entire step (number 27) devoted to *hesychia*, which proved influential over the centuries, especially among the hesychast writers of the fourteenth century who defended this tradition on Mount Athos. The respect for John Climacus is still evident from the unusual prominence that he enjoys in the Orthodox liturgical cycle and by the appointment of the *Ladder* to be read aloud in church or in the refectory, as well as privately, on Mount Athos during Lent. Many older monks will have heard or read the text as many as fifty or sixty times during their lifetime.

In the *Ladder*, John speaks of two levels of silence, an outward ('the door of the cell') and an inward ('the door of the tongue').[4] On the outward level, silence signifies external, physical withdrawal from noise, an outward way of solitude as compared with a communal way of life. In this sense *hesychia* is practised in the eremitic or semi-eremitic forms of monastic life, mostly encountered on the eastern parts of the Athonite peninsula. On the inward level, silence denotes an inner disposition, the spiritual withdrawal from earthly visions and forms. The hesychast is someone concentrated on God. Here hesychia reflects stillness, the goal of every monk on Mount Athos.

The two senses somewhat overlap, but they are not identical. Many hermits may lack internal prayer, while many cenobitic monks may possess inward silence of the heart, unceasing inner prayer. In the sixth century, Abba Barsanuphius observes: 'Silence does not consist of keeping your mouth shut.' One may speak without losing 'silence', while another may say one word and be babbling.[5]

In silence, the power of the soul is confined within the body. The hesychast is not dispersed but concentrated on a single point: God. Therefore, the true definition of silence is not outward but inward: a movement from multiplicity to simplicity, from diversity to unity.[6] 'The kingdom of God is within you' (Luke 17:21). The hesychast realises this truth inwardly and intensely. In this way, silence too connects with apophatic theology, which applies equally to theology as to the life of prayer. God is a mystery beyond understanding and experience. So silence is a fitting way of addressing God in prayer through an image-less, word-less attitude whereby one no longer says prayers but becomes prayer.

On Mount Athos, time and space deliberately allow for this kind of silence. When reading Scripture, the monks do so in silence – whether reading alone in their cells or listening together during meals. They seek to hear the Word of Scripture, and silent reading issues precisely in clear listening. By the same token, when working, they aim to remember in silence God's presence. I recall one monk saying: 'When we prepare meals in the kitchen, we are serving God; when we work in the office, we are signing covenants with God; when we dig the garden, we are actually searching for God.' The work is normally repetitive, rhythmical, undistracting – whether it be woodcarving, washing, fishing or tilling.

God is made present in silence, and the monk becomes present to God in the same sacrament of silence. This presence through silence is pre-eminently realised in the 'pure' or 'noetic (intellectual)' prayer, a way of knowing God's love. 'Prayer of the heart' – another phrase so popular in the fourteenth century – is very much alive on Mount Athos. Heart and mind, body and soul are united in prayer – no longer in opposition one to another (cf. Rom. 7:15–16). The basic words of this prayer, known as the Jesus Prayer, are, 'Lord Jesus Christ, have mercy on me.'[7]

The Jesus Prayer is the way that silent prayer has been

practised for centuries on the Holy Mountain. The origins of this prayer may be sought in Nitria and Scetis of fourth-century Egypt.[8] There, small families of monks and nuns would aim at continual memory of God, whether in common prayer, in private devotion, or in manual labour such as weaving baskets.

The fundamental elements of the Jesus Prayer include the discipline of repetition, the emphasis on penitence, the teaching on imageless prayer, the devotion to the holy name of Jesus, the use of a specific formula (probably dating from the sixth or seventh century), and the linking of this formula with the rhythm of breathing (a technique found as early as the thirteenth century).[9] It is both a formal prayer with a set formula and formatted structure and a freeing prayer, where the monk spends time with self and God. It can be intimidating in its technicalities, but it is a uniquely intimate way of relating to God in all that one does. One lets go of – Evagrius speaks of 'removing' or 'rejecting' – one's expectations of self and God.[10]

THE WAY OF INTEGRITY AND OPENNESS

Silence underlines the aspect of listening, and specifically of listening to another person in obedience. The relationship between spiritual elder and disciple has been fundamental throughout the development of spirituality in the East. It is discussed in a separate chapter below. Nonetheless, it should be noted that the roots of this tradition lie in the New Testament, especially the letters of St Paul (cf. 1 Cor. 4:15), while its fundamental principles are early articulated in formative texts, such as the Sayings of the Desert Fathers. With specific reference to Mount Athos, it should be emphasised that it is the role of the elder, not any rule of the individual, that is of primary significance in Eastern monastic spirituality. In the context of Athos's overpowering millennial tradition, such spiritual direction is a crucial way for preserving personal flexibility as well as integrity.

People will decide to enter a monastery on Mount Athos

after choosing an elder for direction, not an order of life. Indeed, visitors come to the Holy Mountain expecting to find such a person, a person of silence, not of scholarship, a healer and not just a preacher. The implication is that, while we do not come to know God 'at second hand', one who has personal and direct experience of God can assist us in this way of knowledge. Every day, then, the monk opens his heart, 'discloses his thoughts'; everything is revealed in detail. The emphasis is on growth, not on guilt; on progress, not on penitential discipline.

The relationship with one's spiritual elder may include confession in the narrower sacramental sense but is not restricted to it. Many renowned spiritual directors of the Christian monastic tradition were not priests: Antony of Egypt, Benedict of Nursia, John Climacus, Symeon the Pious, Francis of Assisi, and in more recent times Staretz Silouan of Mount Athos (d. 1938) and the Elder Paissios (d. 1994).

On Athos today, it is not uncommon for a monk to approach an unordained, lay monastic elder. The aim is to encounter God at the margins of silence and in the paradox of self-renunciation. To confide is to confess; to confess is to throw off all disguise. Allowing another into one's life is learning to share every thought, feeling, action, insight, wound and joy. To seek God may be an intellectual exercise; to acquire silence may be an individual feat; but to learn to trust another person is to discover all three.

Consultation or confession is to be seen in terms of re-integration, not remorse. Dependence on an elder looks to wholeness in the same way as silence before the 'Other' leads to holiness. The aim is an integrity and integration between what one is and what one does. There is something healing simply in sharing verbally with the elder. The sense of communion, or community, is crucial in this way of life. Doing by sharing is always better than doing alone.

In fact, the entire Mountain of Athos is a community with structures that support individual monasteries and hermits. There is the 'Holy Community', a representative assembly that meets three times weekly, and an *Epistasia*, a kind of executive branch, whose members change each year. Both bodies reside permanently at the Athonite capital, Karyes, where each monastery maintains a residence. Their function varies from retaining the traditions to ratifying regulations, to regulating trade, to reconciling differences, to relating to external authorities (civil and ecclesiastical).

The Athonite community has for centuries zealously guarded its independence, lying as it does under the jurisdiction of the Ecumenical Patriarch in Constantinople (not the Church of Greece), and enjoying privileges of imperial authority in the past and of spiritual autonomy in the present. It is this ideal that produced the many prohibitions in force on Mount Athos, the most ancient and most provocative of which is the prevention of women from even setting foot on the peninsula.

In the late eleventh century, groups of nomadic shepherds settled within the frontiers of the Mountain, pasturing their flocks and trading with the monks. The presence of these people, and especially of women, was disquieting. A description from one monk tells how:

> The devil had entered the hearts of these shepherds who brought their women with them ... The women ... worked for the monasteries, bringing to them cheese and milk and wool, and even baking for the festivals. In brief, they were very much liked by the monks ... And the things that occurred are shameful both to tell and to hear.[11]

'The hesychasts', so it is recorded, 'were disturbed.' The patriarch intervened – for the first time in the history of Athos. Indeed, it is unclear which invasion was more threatening to the monks, that of the women or that of the patriarch! The shepherds were expelled.

Spiritual direction and spiritual freedom are of paramount importance for the Athonite solitaries. Perhaps the greatest contribution of the hesychast tradition is not the technique of silent prayer but the tradition of the spiritual elder. It is in this way, too, that Mount Athos has retained a relationship with the 'outside world', since many monks travel widely to offer such counsel.

CELL AND CELEBRATION

Whether in their cells for private prayer or in church for corporate celebration, the spiritual ideal of the monks does not fundamentally alter. Whether being in worship or simply being, the aim is always silence, a stillness as silent as the flow of blood in our bodies.

This stillness is creative and life-giving. It is an 'ever-moving stillness'.[12] It is not a total absence of sound. There are always many sounds on the mountain of silence: not only the wind and the sea, the birds and the insects, but also the *simantron* or wooden gong, and the bells that call the monks to a chanting that itself never breaks the silence but awakens the whole world to a song.

This is their world of liturgy. After the fourteenth-century triumph of hesychasm, there was a spiritual and cultural explosion, an exporting of monastic ideals throughout the Byzantine world. On Mount Athos, in particular, constitutional charters, liturgical styles and monastic piety were deeply marked by hesychasm. Athonite monks even became candidates for powerful sees. The most celebrated example is Philotheos Kokkinos, formerly abbot of the Great Lavra, who as Ecumenical Patriarch vindicated – and later even canonised – Gregory Palamas, the defender of the Athonite hesychasts.

In total silence and utter darkness, the monks gather inside the central church to celebrate the presence of God. The celebration is more elaborate in larger communities, more simple in smaller sketes. The chant stands out in the omnipresent background of silence. One can truly 'be still, and know God' (Ps. 46:10). Services take place in a dark magnificence of colour, tone and fragrance, over which the candles cast shadows, though little light. As dawn encroaches, sunlight brings shape to pillars as well as to worshippers propped up in their stalls.

The festal services are majestic: whirling chandeliers shine on every icon in the church, wonderful Byzantine chant ranging from the joyful songs of heaven to the nostalgic monotony of a paradise lost. On Sundays and major feast days, monasteries rejoice; food and wine are plentiful; talk flows. But on other days, it is as if time has stopped. On Mount Athos, they keep their own time (Byzantine time, each day starting at sunset), their own calendar (the Julian calendar, thirteen days behind ours), and their own rhythm, so powerful it either sweeps you away or else leaves you behind. The monks feel they have no right to divide time: they do not say 'good morning' or 'good night'. The greeting repeated – morning, afternoon and evening – is 'Bless!' Time is not divided into segments but deified in its entirety. All times are sacred; all moments are lived out in the presence of God.

The daily schedule, too, is a programme of silence:

A bell rings in the silence of the night at about midnight, calling monks to silent prayer and study.

A wooden gong sounds at 4.00 a.m., inviting monks to worship (Matins and Liturgy, normally on a daily basis) in the silence of the night.

The monks proceed silently to the refectory, where:

Lunch follows in silence at 8.00 a.m.

There is a brief period of rest and quiet.

From 10.00 a.m. to 4.00 p.m., the monks work in silence.

Vespers is at 5.00 p.m.

The evening meal, again in silence, is at 6.00 p.m.

There may follow a spell of relaxation from work and silence, when monks mingle with one another or with visitors on the balconies.

Compline in the main church is held at 7.00 p.m.

Afterwards the monks retire in complete silence to their cells.

The entire daily pattern of prayer, work, meals and sleep serves only to punctuate the primacy of silence. Spiritual, physical and social activities are all directed towards, and must never usurp, this end. 'The monk's entire life is a season for prayer.'[13] Signs are posted in the guesthouses: 'Respect the silence.' 'Do not talk after Compline.' Or, 'Do not stay longer than a day.'

THE BODY AND CREATION

Monasticism is closely connected to the practice of asceticism. Asceticism, in turn, involves the renunciation of fleshly desire and even of the flesh. History provides numerous examples of aggression or abuse in this regard. However, at least in its more genuine representatives, asceticism looks to the transformation and not the mortification of the body. On Mount Athos, even after years of harsh and sparse living, monks can be charming, compassionate, accessible and above all tranquil. Neither asceticism nor fasting is to be practised in a way that will insult the Creator of our bodies and of the food that we eat.

Silence, however, is linked with surrendering not what we eat or possess but our very life to God. Silence and death go hand in hand; to be utterly silent can feel like death.[14] On Mount Athos, there is certainly a tradition of silence and death. This is manifested in the veneration of relics, whose inspection may be a frightening prospect to the tourist but whose presence is a treasure for the monks themselves. These relics are the essence of their past and the source of their life.

There is a word, frequently used on the Mountain, which describes silence in life as well as serenity in death. It is *anapausis*, which literally means 'rest' or 'pause'. In the seventh century, Isaac of Syria wrote: 'The silence of the serene is the essence of prayer.'[15] I recall the myth of the Australian thorn bird:

> There is a legend about a bird, which sings just once in its life, more sweetly than any other creature on the face of the earth. From the moment it leaves the nest it searches for a thorn-tree, and does not rest until it has found one. Then, singing among the savage branches, it impales itself upon the longest, sharpest spine. And, dying, it rises above its own agony to out-carol the lark and the nightingale. One superlative song; existence the price. But the whole world stills to listen, and God in His heaven smiles.[16]

One cannot really talk about Mount Athos without some reference also to its natural environment, which in itself is a sacrament of silence and divine presence. Athos is not only a mountain of holy monks, of holy icons, of holy relics and of holy monasteries. It is itself a Holy Mountain. The whole peninsula is the context of sacred space. As an elderly Russian monk used to say, 'Here, every stone breathes prayer.'[17]

The intrinsic sacredness of the mountain is again reflected in its stillness, which is everywhere and pervades everything: the sea, the snow-peaked Athos, the forests, the paths, the wildlife, shrubs and flowers. The ringing of the bells, the rustling of a lizard, the distant sound of a motorboat, and the noise of more recent technology – all emphasise, even by their interruption, the intensity of quiet.

There is a quaint Athonite anecdote that relates the disturbance of the monks' morning prayer by the noise of the frogs in the cistern outside their chapel. The elder of the skete went out and rebuked them severely: 'Frogs, would you mind keeping quiet? We've just ended the Midnight Office and are about to start Matins.' To this the frogs replied: 'Perhaps it is you who should be keeping quiet. We've just ended Matins and are moving on to Liturgy!' The silence of the monks and the sound of creation ultimately share the same language.

It is at night, however, that the mountain is especially deep in prayer, sharing the anguish of the whole creation: the aged hands of the hermits uplifted, the younger monks rising from prostrations, the priests raising the holy gifts. Everything is directed upwards, just like the vertical prayer of the forest, the precipitous rise of the rocks, and the high splashing of the waves.

Much as creation groans in pain when we relate to it irresponsibly, so also must it rejoice in silence when we treat it properly. While many of the younger monks have brought with them the modern technology of their urban background, hopefully ecological sensitivity will continue to be maintained.

CONCLUSION

Today there are over two thousand monks on Mount Athos. Twenty-five years ago the average age was over sixty, while today most are younger than forty. It is inappropriate to compare the higher education of the younger monks with the humble simplicity of former generations. Yet the fervour is very much alive and the change most welcome.

Over the centuries, the Holy Mountain has produced numerous saints (martyrs, monastics and even missionaries) of the Orthodox calendar (there is even a Sunday dedicated to their collective memory in the Orthodox Church, the first Sunday after the Easter cycle); it has presented many spiritual writers (Gregory Palamas, as well as Kallistos and Ignatios Xanthopouloi, from the great period of the hesychasts, but more recently Nikodemus the Hagiorite [d. 1809]); it can boast masterful iconography (by Manuel Panselinos in the thirteenth century, by Theophanes the Cretan in the sixteenth). The twentieth century has seen fine examples in all three of these areas.

So, while rejecting the world, the silence of Mount Athos indicates that there is a world beyond the one we have fashioned for ourselves. In Palladius' *Lausiac History*, Macarius the Great is described as 'holding up the walls'.[18] In many ways, the monks of Mount Athos are today holding up the walls of centuries-old monasteries, preserving age-old manuscripts and icons, maintaining traditional ways. Yet above and beyond these, the monks of Athos alert us to the centre of the world that holds together all things. John Climacus writes: 'The one who has achieved silence has arrived at the very centre of all mysteries.'[19] Centredness is an appropriate way of describing the monastic life on Athos. Centredness is also a fitting definition of prayerful silence, as it has been experienced through the centuries in the Athonite tradition.

6. PATHS OF CONTINUITY: CONTEMPORARY WITNESSES OF THE HESYCHAST EXPERIENCE

> To think about God a thousand times, without experiencing God, is to know nothing. (Gregory Palamas)

> The saints are our theologians. (Abbot Vasileios of Iveron)

When exploring the Christian East, it is critical to examine it in the context of a living tradition. Behind each representative, there stands an uninterrupted path of continuity. We do not do proper justice to authors such as the desert fathers and mothers (fourth to fifth centuries), John Climacus (d. *c.* 649), Symeon the New Theologian (d. 1049) or Gregory Palamas (d. 1359) unless we study them in light of 'a cloud of witnesses' (Heb. 12:1) – at once known and unknown, both men and women, early and medieval and modern alike – who both pursued and paved the same way to the heart.

The three figures portrayed in this chapter lived recently on Mount Athos. They complement one another: Sophrony analysed the Jesus Prayer and its methodology; Joseph made the Jesus Prayer his unceasing activity; and, while Paisios hardly mentioned the Jesus Prayer, it was clearly the source of all that he did. Each of them played a critical role in the revival of the monastic ideal in the twentieth century. They reflect the diversity of the heart's ways and the breadth of desert spirituality, alive today no less than in the past.

THE WISDOM OF THE HEART: SOPHRONY OF ESSEX (1896–1993)

Archimandrite Sophrony Sakharov[1] was born Sergei Symeonovich in Tsarist Russia in 1896 and studied fine arts in Moscow, where he developed an interest in Buddhism and Indian culture. With the outbreak of World War I and the subsequent Revolution in Russia, Sophrony meditated on the cause of suffering and the source of truth.

By 1921, Sophrony had emigrated to Europe, travelling through Italy and Germany to France, where he exhibited his work in prestigious salons. He soon lost interest in matters purely intellectual, enrolling in the Orthodox Theological Institute of St Serge in Paris. He abandoned these studies to make his way to St Panteleimon Monastery on Mount Athos.

In 1930, Sophrony encountered Staretz Silouan whom he acclaimed as the greatest gift from God. For eight years, Sophrony enjoyed the spiritual direction of this *staretz* (the Russian word for 'elder'), until – on his death (in 1938) – he departed the monastery for the 'desert' of the Holy Mountain.

It was not long before Sophrony was called to serve as spiritual advisor to several communities of the Holy Mountain. He also moved to a more remote region of the Athonite 'desert', where he inhabited a small chapel (10' x 7') hewn out of the rock face. There, he endured rigorous conditions (no fire, and much dampness) for a life of reading and prayer. After three winters, failing health obliged him to relinquish the cave and he travelled once again to France, where surgery crushed any hope of returning to Athos. There, he recorded the biographical details and spiritual teachings of his *staretz*. In 1952, Sophrony published *The Undistorted Image*,[2] the story of Staretz Silouan. The *staretz* was widely acknowledged as a spiritual heir to the great teachers of the paths to the heart and 'canonised' by the official Church in 1988. In 1958, Sophrony founded a small community in Essex, England, where he died in 1993.

In another book, *His Life Is Mine*,[3] Sophrony reveals certain illuminating insights into themes such as divine knowledge, light and vision, as well as the way that leads to these: struggle, prayer and repentance. Sophrony is aware that spiritual knowledge is 'preserved and handed on . . . from generation to generation'.[4] His own foundation and roots clearly lie in *the tradition of Mount Athos*, which he explicitly acknowledges: 'This is the great culture of the heart I met with on the Holy Mountain.'[5] Sophrony refers to the never-ending growth of the soul which, 'as a matter of course, aspires to ever deeper knowledge'.[6] 'There is', he says, 'no end to this learning'[7] – echoing the tradition of spiritual authors who speak of *epektasis*, of unending perfection. And, while he desires to communicate the beauty of this experience, he confesses that it is 'impossible to keep silent; impossible to give voice'[8] – again in succession of spiritual authors who refer to *apophasis*, to the negative way.

The human person is a mystery. Sophrony speaks of 'man as being indeed an enigma'.[9] '[Man] is more than a microcosm – he is a microtheos.'[10] The human heart is a mystery in the 'image and likeness of God' (Gen. 1:26). 'The heart is deep' (Ps. 63:7). For Sophrony, this mystical dimension of the heart is both central and critical. As the meeting-point between God and the world, the heart is the place where the divine light is beheld: 'God reveals Himself, mainly through the heart, as Love and Light.'[11] This divine light is real, not an imaginary figment or figure of speech. Sophrony represents here the *'mystics of light'*, a tradition dominant in the Christian East. He stands alongside Origen (second to third centuries), Evagrius (fourth century), the desert fathers (fourth to fifth centuries), the *Homilies* attributed to Macarius (fourth to fifth centuries), Diadochus (fifth century) and John Climacus (seventh century), a line continued right up to Symeon the New Theologian (eleventh century) and Gregory Palamas (fourteenth century).

The 'depth of illumination' is found in love, which 'shines in our hearts', 'a light shining in a dark place' (2 Cor. 4:6; 2 Peter 1:19). The notion of 'the eyes of [one's] understanding being enlightened' (Eph. 1:8) expresses an idea central with Sophrony:

> Sometimes prayer consumes the heart like fire; and when
> the heart succumbs to the burning flame, unexpectedly

there falls the dew of divine consolation. When we become
so conscious of our frailty that our spirit despairs, somehow, in an unknown fashion, a wondrous light appears,
proclaiming life incorruptible. When the darkness within
us is so appalling that we are paralyzed with dread, the
same light will turn black night into bright day . . . When
we are overwhelmed by the feeling of our own utter noth-
ingness, the uncreated light transfigures and brings us
like sons into the Father's house.[12]

Sophrony adopts the image of a centuries-old tree whose roots
must lie deep in the earth if its branches are to reach up to the
clouds.[13] The whole human person, including the body, shines if
the heart is illumined (Prov. 15:13). This is no natural light,
unlike any personal gift or artistic talent. Sophrony is convinced that it is supernatural: 'He who accepts it knows from
whence it came – knows whether it was pronounced of man or
whether it did verily come down "from the Father of Lights"
(Jas. 1:17).'[14]

On the one hand, the heart's function is *ascetical*: it is a
struggle to attain to spiritual liberty. For Sophrony, the sign of
this freedom of the Spirit is, first, 'a disinclination to impose
one's will on others' and, second, 'an inner release from the
hold of others on oneself'.[15] Such liberation, or revelation,
comes only 'after long years of ascetic striving'.[16] On the other
hand, the heart's function is *liturgical*: as a unifying organ, it
offers up the entire human person to God. Sophrony declares:
'The priest's whole being – heart, mind, body – must unite in
sorrowful prayer for the world.'[17] The liturgy of the priest is of
course more than 'simply a form of psychological or mental
"remembering"'; it is the preservation and continuation of
knowledge through 'generations of priests'.[18] The ascetical and
the liturgical dimensions coincide in prayer, which is 'an
infinite creation, a supreme art'.[19] Indeed, many of the chapters
in his book open with a creative and poetic prayer by the Elder,
who boldly introduced personal prayers into his celebration of
the Divine Liturgy.

Two final points should be highlighted. First, while in Sophrony's books – unlike the writings of Philo the Jew (first century), Clement of Alexandria (third century), Gregory of Nyssa (fourth century) and Dionysius the Areopagite (*c.* 500) – there are no traces of any 'mysticism of darkness', there is a great deal of emphasis on *the significance of suffering*. It is a suffering of the heart, or 'broken-heartedness' (Ps. 50:17). For Sophrony, 'through suffering we penetrate the mysteries of Being'.[20] He devotes the entire thirteenth chapter to 'the prayer of Gethsemane'. Ultimately, all suffering is contained and comprehended on the cross:

> This spiritual vision . . . dissolves into contemplation of the crucified Christ. The way to this . . . lies through the depths of hell . . . The hands of Christ crucified link the far ends of the abyss . . . Thus the first dread vision of darkness and mortality changes to a vision of light and life indestructible. [Then,] the touch of divine love in the heart is our first contact with the heavenly side of the abyss.[21]

Even the physical heart feels this sensation of pain within the arduous act of prayer:

> This concentration within may take the form of a cramp whereby heart, mind and body are contracted together, like a tightly clenched fist. Prayer becomes a wordless cry, and regret for the distance separating him from God turns to acute grief.[22]

And, although at the outset of the path, 'now there is suffering and now rejoicing', at the final destination:

> There is no more alternating between elation and depression, since all states are gathered into a single whole. Through knowledge of God the soul has acquired profound peace.[23]

Second, Sophrony believes that 'when God by the Holy Spirit gives us understanding, our *prayer assumes cosmic propor-*

tions'. And, although it is not always clear whether these proportions extend beyond '[hu]mankind'[24], the implication is that 'the intrinsic quality of life is enhanced' and 'everything that happens will take on a different character'.[25] So, knowledge of God involves contemplation of the world.[26] Darkness and 'death engulf all creation, ourselves first and foremost'.[27] So too does God's light and life:

> When you feel the touch of the Eternal Spirit in your heart . . . love streams like a light on all creation. Though the physical heart feels this love, in kind it is spiritual – metaphysical . . . Yet only those . . . who keep a clear conscience not only before God but toward their neighbor, towards animals – even towards the material things which are the product of men's labor – will care for all creation . . . [Love] embraces all created beings in joy over their salvation . . . For the Divine Spirit draws the heart to compassion for all creation.[28]

Such is the path that Sophrony learned directly through the inspiration of his elder, Staretz Silouan, who taught him – in his now classic exhortation – to 'stay his mind in hell and despair not':

> We are naturally attracted to the All-Highest, but our pilgrimage must start with a descent into the pit of hell. Then we are nearing the end of our long search to discover the depth of Being.[29]

THE DEPTH OF THE HEART: JOSEPH THE HESYCHAST (1898–1959)

The biography of Elder Joseph the Hesychast describes him as a 'legitimate continuator of the patristic tradition'.[30] It is recorded by Joseph the younger (b. 1921), who lived for twelve years with his spiritual father until the latter's death in 1959. Joseph the Hesychast was born in 1898 on the small island of Paros in Greece. Orphaned as a young child, Joseph (né

Francis) began to work from a tender age in order to assist his family. At the age of twenty-three, he came across the writings of the Church Fathers and decided to pursue the monastic path. He made his way to Athens where he met with Athonite monks whom he followed to the Holy Mountain. There he sought to learn about silence and attentiveness in a variety of persons and lifestyles.

One day, filled with tears, he prayed to the Mother of God:

> At last, I was completely changed, and forgot myself. I was filled with light in my heart and outside and everywhere, not being aware that I even had a body. The 'prayer' [that is, the Jesus Prayer] began to say itself within me so rhythmically that I was amazed, since I myself was not making any effort.[31]

It was not long before Arsenios (d. 1984), a monk from Stavronikita Monastery, became his inseparable companion and ascetic partner in the search for silence. Joseph was enthusiastic about the inner way of the heart. He would pray for long hours, silently sitting in a remote cave on a small wooden stool and keeping his mind in his heart. He fasted intensely (eating only three ounces of food near the time of sunset) and kept extended vigil. He continued wandering the Mountain for eight years, finally settling in the Skete of St Basil. He practised no handiwork, so as not to distract from his concentration on prayer. His ascetic discipline included standing upright for long periods.

Yet no matter how austere Joseph was to himself, he understood well that monastic perfection was to be found not in outward ascetic feats or rigorous deprivations, but in the inward life of the monk, hidden in silence and cultivated in stillness. The Hesychast would later teach his disciples 'to stay within [their] own measure, and not extend [themselves] beyond [their] strength'.[32]

From St Basil's Skete, Joseph and Arsenios moved to a small region in Little St Anne. There, the two ascetics lived in three small cells (6' x 5'): one for each of them, and one for the visiting clergyman who celebrated the liturgy. After attracting a small number of close disciples, and out of concern for their health, Joseph encouraged Arsenios to make a last move, this time to New Skete (in 1951). There, after falling ill on the eve of New Year 1958, and following a painful few months, Joseph prepared for his death by fasting of everything except holy communion for almost forty days, the last of his earthly life. On 15 August 1959, on the Feast of his beloved Mother of God, Joseph was seated in liturgy when he passed into the heavenly age.

For the Hesychast Joseph, *the way of the ascetics is the way of obedience*. 'There is no other road to salvation like this,' he writes.[33] Yet, while obedience is a mystery, it is not magical; Joseph's teaching is quite radical: 'As I have said before, the divine will with its transcendent character is not magically contained within positions or places or instruments.' He does not recommend a slavish adherence to a set of regulations or doctrines. Often Joseph will say: 'Do as you think best.'[34] The ascetic discipline is closely related to spiritual disciple-ing: disobedience implies disorder; obedience includes a 'regime' of prayer and struggle. Joseph's way was identified with that of the Fathers: 'Testing and experience have convinced me to act in this way . . . This is the common path of the Fathers.' In all things, the question on his mind and to his disciples was forward-looking: 'Where is God?' The 'new creation', as he called it, was always the spiritual focus of the elder.[35]

Joseph the Hesychast decried the dangerous '"fashion" of self-appointed experts speaking about mental prayer, the uncreated light, deification and the like'.[36] The notion of tradition was the only safeguard against this danger, and so Joseph continually refers to the Church Fathers, virtually on every page quoting from the writings of the *Philokalia*. Joseph believed that 'if such people as continue this tradition disappear, then the end of this world will come'.

While reverence to tradition is important for Joseph, *the rigour or violence of ascetic struggle* is the most striking aspect of his spiritual way. 'The right use of conceptual images follows the right use of things.'[37] Indeed, the way that we regard our world is reflected in the way that we treat our world. Joseph learned the 'almost indistinguishable' details and trials, the various changes and dispositions, of the spiritual struggle: 'As night follows day, so successes are followed by trials that test us ... The main path is the martyrdom of our conscience ... and unceasing self-denial.'[38] This was a struggle he undertook and understood personally:

> If you are going to lose grace and not know how to recall it, I prefer you not to find it, however harsh this may seem. This is why I wish you experience rather than grace. Experience brings many graces and recalls them if they hide themselves, but premature grace brings no experience.[39]

The spiritual struggle, however, is not a way of personal triumph or achievement. Rather, for Joseph, it is *a way of sharing through suffering*. The spiritual law of suffering is a reality whereby we assume responsibility for affliction in the world.[40] Exposure to trials (*peirasmoi*) engenders experience (*peira*) in 'bearing one another's burdens' (Gal. 6:2). Passion is ultimately a way to com-passion. The aim is to endure patiently the spiritual warfare until the very wounds of the heart and the weaknesses of the world are transformed.[41]

'The dogma of love', then, transcends and exceeds 'the law of duty'.[42] The ascetic reaches the point where 'he neither blames nor condemns anyone for anything, not even Satan himself'.[43] The opposite – and enemy – of love is self-love, expressed as the vice of negligence and caused by the 'complications of indifference'.[44] The cure for negligence is remembrance of the kingdom. Love is impossible without complete obedience; and prayer is impossible without true love.[45]

Nevertheless, spiritual struggle is not an end in itself; 'the battle against the passions is the beginning of the path to pure prayer ... The work of prayer ... is superior to every virtue and commandment.'[46] Prayer of the heart always remained 'the chief preoccupation and the chief goal' of the Elder,[47] who has more to say about the stages of the struggle to regain purity of heart than he has to say about the ideal or final condition of the heart. He feels more comfortable admitting that the heart is a mystery – 'beyond speech, beyond substance, ungraspable, contained only to the extent that it itself extends the mind'.[48] And he understands the purpose of prayer as being love, a goal achievable by every person under any conditions and in all circumstances.[49]

Then, as he writes, 'created things are reconnected with their Creator'.

> When grace is operative in the soul of someone who is praying, then that person is flooded with the love of God, so that he can no longer bear what he experiences. Afterwards, this love turns towards the world and man . . . In general he suffers with every grief and misery, *even for the dumb animals*, so that he weeps when he thinks that they are suffering. These are properties of love, but it is prayer that activates them and calls them forth. That is why those who are advanced in prayer do not cease to pray for the world. To them belongs even the continuation of life, however strange and audacious this may seem.[50]

THE BREADTH OF THE HEART: PAISIOS THE ELDER (1924–94)

Elder Paisios was born in 1924 in Cappadocia, Asia Minor, a region traditionally renowned for its Byzantine heritage and popular piety. He was baptised by his village priest, Fr Arsenios (d. 1924), receiving the name Arsenios.[51] That priest was recently recognised as a saint in the Orthodox Church (1988). Paisios' family fled as refugees from Asia Minor to Greece where they first settled on the island of Corfu and finally in the north-eastern town of Konitsa in Epirus.[52] There, Paisios completed his elementary education and military service.

In 1950, a year after military discharge, Paisios left for

Mount Athos where he submitted to the spiritual guidance of a monk named Cyril and received his monastic tonsure and name, Averkios. His favourite reading included *The Sayings of the Desert Fathers* and Abba Isaac the Syrian, whose *Mystic Treatises* he kept beneath his pillow at all times.[53] Four years later, he received his monastic habit (or *schema*) and the new name Paisios. In 1962, Paisios travelled to Mount Sinai, where he remained for two years in a mountainous cell opposite the holy mount of the Burning Bush and St Catherine's Monastery. The Bedouins loved Paisios, who used to carve wooden crosses and sell them to pilgrims in order to buy food for the natives.

In 1964, he returned to the Holy Mountain, where he settled in the Skete of Iviron. His spiritual father during this period was a charismatic Russian elder named Tychon (1884–1968). In 1968, Paisios encouraged one of his closest disciples to serve as Abbot in order to restore Stavronikita Monastery, a step that proved critical and formative in the recent revival of monasticism on the Holy Mountain.

In 1979, Paisios moved to 'Panagouda' (or 'little Virgin Mother'), which was to be the last cell that he inhabited on the Mountain. From here, he directed the lives of numerous people who sought his advice through visitations and correspondence alike. In a small bottle with paper and pencil, outside the fence that surrounded his cell, people would leave notes with personal problems, names of those seeking intercession, letters requiring counsel, and gifts for distribution to the poor. Paisios literally became a magnet that drew out and transformed human pain and suffering.

In 1966, he began to experience problems with his respiratory system. During one of his hospitalisations in Thessalonika, the Elder became acquainted with the Convent of St John the Theologian at Souroti, a small town outside of Thessalonika. When in 1988, Paisios' health had deteriorated irreparably – diagnosed with liver and lung cancer – it was the nuns of this convent who nursed him. He died on 12 July 1994.

Paisios sensed himself as *part of a long spiritual tradition*, not only because of the holy man who baptised him but also because of the holy mountain where he dwelt. Yet for him, tradition is more than a mere historical lineage; it implies an *unbroken sacramental heritage*: 'We are in no way inferior to the Apostles [he observes]. The Apostles were physically close to Christ . . . However, we, too, have Him inside our soul from a very young age, through the grace of Holy Baptism.'[54] He did not simply belong to a tradition; he incarnated the convictions of that tradition: 'I do not care any more if someone tells me that God does not exist!'[55] This is because he knows personally!

Paisios is also one of the few ascetics – of the contemporary present or even the classic past – who refers to the sacraments, and especially to Baptism: 'The grace of God entered our soul through Holy Baptism; it is a gift granted to all of us.'[56]

Grace constitutes the starting-point and goal of ascetic discipline. The aim of self-purification is to allow more room for divine grace: *ascesis* looks to *kenosis*. Or, put differently, *labora* leads to *ora*: 'Do your spiritual work,' he recommends, 'and say the Jesus Prayer. Your thoughts, will, and desires are where your mind is.'[57] The purpose of ascetic renunciation is 'to count down from ten to zero before sending off our missile into space! – like the Americans do!'[58] He strongly advises people to 'live as simply as they can', not allowing their lives to become complicated.[59]

Perhaps the most apparent feature is his positive and edifying counsel. His spirituality resembles that of the desert fathers, with their emphasis on honesty and integrity. 'Be who you are' is the advice he often gives people who approach him; 'do not pretend'.[60] His was a *positive spirituality*. Paisios believed that positive thoughts beget positive thoughts:

> Think positively. Try to develop positive thoughts. It is more important for one to develop good thoughts than to be guided by a spiritual father who is considered a living saint. A single positive thought equals a vigil [i.e., an entire night in prayer] on Mount Athos.[61]

He is at home with the ways and wiles of the thoughts:

> I know from experience that in this life people are divided
> into two categories. A third category does not exist; peo-
> ple either belong to one or another. The first resembles
> the fly. The main characteristic of the fly is that it is
> attracted to dirt . . . The other category is like the bee,
> whose main characteristics always to look for something
> sweet.[62]

Ultimately, Paisios has a sound knowledge of his own heart
and mind:

> It is much better to be aware of our own weakness, than
> to struggle very hard while neglecting it . . . I have been
> a monk for many years and among the virtues I have
> acquired, I have also developed some weaknesses, which
> I have not managed to get rid of.[63]

However, his is not simply a spirituality of 'feeling good' or
'self-help'. Paisios is careful to underline the importance of
guidance in thoughts: 'You can turn the wheel [of thoughts],
but your spiritual father will show you the direction.'[64]

Paisios further qualifies his 'positive spirituality' by adopt-
ing an *apophatic* attitude. He insists that the 'soul must be
cleansed from positive thoughts as well':[65]

> We must not have any thoughts in our mind or heart,
> neither positive ones nor negative ones, for this space
> inside us belongs to the grace of God. We must ignore
> both positive and negative thoughts, and always confess
> them to our spiritual father, and obey whatever he tells
> us.[66]

Reference here to God's grace leads to another fundamental
element in Paisios' teaching, namely the emphasis on *grace or
gratitude*. Without this particular element, Paisios says, 'we do
not only not seek divine assistance, but we also misuse our
own logic'.[67] In fact, lack of gratitude for God's grace leads to
grief; the vocation of human beings is to be 'filled with responsive gratefulness'![68]

Finally, while positive thinking may reflect one aspect of Paisios' spiritual teaching, *spiritual practicality* reflects another. He is balanced in his outlook, even in matters of prayer and discipline:

> Everything must be done with discretion. We should not indiscreetly hold long services that make most of the monks fall asleep. During vigils, we should take into consideration both the younger monks, who are still weak, and the older ones.[69]

The 'practical' matters broached by the Elder include: taking medication (he says that 'pills will not solve the problem, but only temporarily cover it'), problems of the church hierarchy (he advises us to 'mind our own humble thoughts'), ecumenism, extraterrestrial creatures (he advises not to worry about them!), voting and taxes, questions about raising children (he observes that children should only be scolded in the morning so as to have the entire day to take their minds *off* the discipline! Paisios also notes: 'While children are young, they are like angels; when they enter their teens . . . they become small beasts!'), getting good grades at school, finding a spiritual father, obedience to spiritual elders and bishops (the latter, he remarks tongue in cheek, we should obey 'with discretion'!), dealing with magic, doctors and obstetricians, cursing, material things, abortion, disability, lying, business, mobile phones (he feels these disturb the silence of the Mountain), fear of war, the rule of prayer, the life of the sacraments, and patience:

> Live with patience, because there is no other way to get through life today. Be patient, and do not take everything too seriously. Go to a large super-market, and buy yourself a good dose of apathy![70]

The realism of his teaching stems from a *sense of compassion*, which allows the Elder to remain deeply connected with society even while separated in monastic isolation.[71] Paisios is anxious to stress personal freedom and responsibility in the struggle against evil and injustice. The passions are not to be destroyed, but restrained and redirected:

> Evil does not exist in this world. Everything was created by God and created 'good' . . . Evil exists when we make wrong use of the things God granted to us for our benefit . . . Therefore, we must use everything in the right way, the natural way, and not abuse them or go against nature.[72]

When one contains the passions, one gains a sense of compassion, which is none other than the experience of divine justice or the vision of the world through the eyes of God. Then one shares 'God's sympathy towards humanity', 'God's providence for the whole creation', and 'God's joy over the repentance even of the devil'. Compassion is another way of giving and of monastic renunciation. Put simply, 'God tolerates everybody.' So too should we![73] Paisios was convinced that, if people 'applied to their lives the things they understand' from the Scriptures, then there would be greater affinities between Christians and adherents of other authentic religions. After all, don't religions seek to love God, to love neighbour and to endure with patience?[74]

Paisios wanted – and encouraged others – to participate in people's problems and pain: 'When we are awake at night praying, we should ask God to help those who suffer from insomnia and require sleeping pills.'[75] The imagery he adopts is preciously simple, reminiscent of the desert fathers: '[Divine] justice is like a cork; no matter how hard we press it to the bottom of the sea, it will always come back to the surface.'[76]

This lens of 'divine sympathy' or 'divine justice' further enables Paisios to feel close to the animal world. His life is replete with stories of intimate connection to animals. This affection – the development of what he calls 'a different attitude inside the soul' – comes less from a sense of abstract identity, as it does from profound humility, obedience and silence. A heart listening humbly to God listens also to God in others and in everything:

> My mind tells me that even animals are better than I; so,
> I humble myself before them and obey them . . . What do
> you think then? Should I obey the animals or not? My
> thoughts tell me that I should.[77]

Paisios even encourages people to write on environmental issues: 'Ecological destruction is taking place. Those who can should write and talk about it!'[78] Such an attitude, caused by the softening of the heart, results in the 'partial experience in this life of heaven or hell'. According to one's clean or unclean conscience, the heart becomes either a place of paradise or else of torment.[79]

CONCLUSION

These three monastic elders embrace a tradition they at once deeply respect and genuinely reflect. Yet, the manner in which they embody and succeed this very tradition differs greatly. One is educated, able to articulate the subtle nuances of the spiritual way; another is unlettered and austere, willing to share the fruits of his rigorous ascetic discipline; the third is a simple, yet popular spiritual guide, able to touch the lives of countless people.

Moreover, while in their solitude living apart from the world, each of these elders remained an integral part of the world, comprised the very heart of the world. It is not the great individual fast or the personal ascetic feat, but the heart of what really matters that counted in their lives. They were pursuers of depth in detail: Sophrony took the time to look you deep in the eyes; Joseph ignored his disability to pick up a mere lentil from the floor; and Paisios conversed with a tiny lizard on his porch.

7. THE BOOK OF NATURE: THEOLOGY, ECOLOGY AND SPIRITUALITY

My book is the nature of created things; there, I can read the works of God. (Antony of Egypt)

An immense cathedral, the universe of God. (Paul Evdokimov)

Whenever we think of the Genesis account of creation, we tend to forget our connection to the earth and our environment. Perhaps it is a natural reaction; or perhaps it is a sign of our arrogance, that we tend to overemphasise our creation 'in the image and likeness of God' (Gen. 1:26) and overlook our creation from the dirt and 'the dust of the ground' (Gen. 2:7). Our 'heavenliness' should not overshadow our 'earthliness'. Most people may be unaware that we human beings did not get a day to ourselves in Genesis. In fact, we shared the sixth day with the creeping and crawling things of the world (Gen. 1:2–26). There is a binding unity and continuity that we share with all of God's creation. Indeed, the depth of Adam (*haadam*) is originally created from and deeply correlated to the topsoil of the earth (*adamah*). It is helpful to recall this truth.

In recent years, we have been reminded – indeed, in a painful way – of this reality with the cruel flora and fauna extinction, with the irresponsible soil and forest clearance, and with the unacceptable noise, air and water pollution. Yet our concern for the environment is not a form of superficial or sentimental love. It is a way of honouring and dignifying our very creation by the hand and word of God. It is a way of listening to 'the mourning of the land' (Hos. 41:3) and 'the groaning of creation' (Rom. 8:22). This chapter is dedicated to the wholeness of truth experienced on that sixth day of creation. Anything less than the full story, any deviation from the fullness of that truth, is a dangerous heresy.[1]

Speaking about heresy when it comes to assessing the environmental crisis is not too far-fetched. Whenever we speak (whether about things in heaven or on earth), we are always drawing upon established values of ourselves and of our world. The technical language that we adopt, and even the particular 'species' that we wish to preserve, all depend on the values and the images that we promote, or rather presume. In Orthodox spirituality, symbols and images certainly play a significant role. When I consider images, I think of the central importance of:

- *icons* (i.e., the way we view and perceive creation);

- *liturgy* (i.e., the way we celebrate and respond to creation); and

- *asceticism* (i.e., the way we respect and treat creation).

A sense of the holy in nature implies that everything that lives is holy. Everything that breathes praises God (Ps. 150:6); the entire world is a 'burning bush of God's energies', as Gregory Palamas stated in the fourteenth century. If we are still, if we grow sensitive, then 'our eyes are opened to see the beauty of created things'.[2] Seeing clearly is precisely what icons teach us to do.

THE ICONIC VISION OF NATURE

As already observed, icons, or sacred images, bear a central importance in Christian Orthodox thought and spirituality. The world of the icon offers new insights, new perceptions into reality. It reveals the eternal dimension in everything that we see and experience in our environment. Our generation, it may be said, is characterised by a sense of self-centredness towards the natural cosmos, by a lack of awareness of or communication with the beyond. We appear to be inexorably locked within the confines of our individual concerns – even in our desire to escape from this impasse – with no access to the world outside or around us. We have broken the sacred covenant, the symbolical connection between our selves and our world.

Well, the icon restores; it reconciles. The icon reminds us of another way and reflects another world. It offers a corrective to the culture that we have created, which gives value only to the here and now. The icon aspires to reveal the inner vision of all, the world as created and as intended by God. Very often, it is said, the first image attempted by an iconographer is that of the transfiguration of Christ on Mount Tabor. This is precisely because the iconographer struggles to hold together this world and the next, to transfigure this world in light of the next. By disconnecting this world from heaven, we have in fact desacralised both. The icon articulates with theological conviction our faith in the heavenly kingdom. The icon does away with any objective distance between this world and the next, between material and spiritual, between body and soul, time and eternity, creation and divinity. The icon reminds us that there is no double vision, no double order in creation. It speaks in this world the language of the age to come.

This is why the doctrine of the divine incarnation, the divine economy, the 'plan' of reconciliation, is at the very heart of iconography. In the icon of Jesus Christ, the uncreated God assumes a creaturely face, a beauty that is exceeding (Ps. 44:2), a 'beauty that can save the world'.[3] And in Orthodox icons, the faces – whether of Christ or of the saints in communion with Christ – are always frontal, depicted with two eyes gazing back at the beholder. The conviction is that Christ is in our midst, here, Emmanuel (Matt. 1:23). Profile signifies sin; it implies a rupture in communication or communion. Faces are frontal, all eyes, eternally receptive and susceptive of divine grace. 'I see' means that 'I am seen', which in turn means that I am in communion. This is the powerful experience of the invisible and the immortal, a passing over to another way of seeing. This is 'Passover', *Pascha*. It is resurrection.

The icon converts the beholder from a restricted, limited point of view to a fuller, spiritual vision, where we see every-thing as reconciled and as united in a single reality, 'in him through whom all things live, move, and have their being' (Acts 17:28). For the light of the icon is the light of reconciliation, the light of restoration, the light of the resurrection. It is not the waning light of this world; it 'knows no evening', to quote an Orthodox hymn. This is why icons depicting events that occurred in the daytime are no brighter than icons depicting events that occurred at night-time. The icon of Gethsemane, for example, is no darker than the icon of Pentecost. The icon of the resurrection is no brighter than the icon of the crucifixion. The icon presupposes, indeed proposes, another light in which to see things, a 'different way of life', as the Orthodox Easter liturgy proclaims. This is a vision that liber-ates us from every alien vision. It provides for us another means of communication, beyond the conceptual, beyond the written, beyond the spoken word. This is the language of silence and of mystery, the language of the kingdom to come.

The entire world is an icon, a door, a window, a point of entry, opening up to a new reality.[4] Everything in this world is a sign, a seed. 'Nothing is a vacuum in the face of God,' wrote Irenaeus of Lyons in the second century; 'everything is a sign of God'. Everything and everyone contains this dimension, bears this transparency. And so in icons, rivers assume human form; so, too, do the sun and the moon and the stars and the waters. All of these assume human faces; all of them acquire a personal dimension – just like people; just like God.

And if the earth is an icon, if this world is an image that reflects the presence of God, then nothing whatsoever can be neutral, nothing at all lacks sacredness. No land is *terra incognita*. The Christian is simply the one who discerns and encounters Christ everywhere, the one who recognises the whole world as the dwelling-place of Christ. For if God were not visible in creation, then neither could God be worshipped as invisible in heaven.

THE LITURGY OF NATURE

What the Orthodox icon does in space and matter, the Christian Orthodox liturgy effects in praise and time: namely the same ministry of reconciliation, the anticipation and participation of heaven on earth. If we are guilty of relentless waste, it is perhaps because we have lost the spirit of worship. We are no longer respectful pilgrims on this earth; we have been reduced to mere tourists.

We have already introduced the world of liturgy; this section will, therefore, concentrate solely on the environmental perspectives of liturgy. The Eastern Orthodox Church retains a liturgical view of the created world, proclaiming a world imbued by God and a God involved in this world. Our original sin, so it seems, lies in our prideful refusal to receive the world as a gift of reconciliation, humbly to regard the world as a sacrament of communion. At a time when we have polluted the air that we breathe and the water that we drink, we are called to restore within ourselves the sense of awe and delight, to respond to matter as to a mystery of ever-increasing connections.

By liturgical, however, I do not imply ritual. I mean movement, dynamism and creativity. The world is not static, as Plato might have believed; nor again is it eternally reproduced, as the classical world-view might have proposed. It is a movement towards an end, towards a final purpose, towards a sacred goal. It is neither endless, nor purposeless. It is essentially relational. To adopt the concept of icons, we are to think of the world too as a picture, as an image: one requires every part of a picture for it to be complete, from the Alpha to the Omega. If one were to move (or to remove, still more so, to destroy) one part of the picture – whether a tree, or an animal, or a human being – then the entire picture would be affected (or distorted, perhaps even destroyed).

The truth is that we respond to nature with the same delicacy, the very same sensitivity, and exactly the same tenderness with which we respond to any human person in a relationship. We have learned not to treat people like things; we must now learn not to treat even things like mere things. All of our ecological activities are measured ultimately by their effect on people, especially upon the poor. And all of our spiritual activities are judged by their impact on our world, especially upon the environment.

Therefore, liturgy is a commemoration of the innate connection between God and people and things. It is a celebration of the sense of communion, this dance of life. When we enter this interdependence of all persons and all things – this 'cosmic liturgy', as St Maximus the Confessor described it – then we can begin to understand the environmental crisis, and to resolve issues of ecology or of economy. In the seventh century, St Isaac the Syrian described this as acquiring 'a merciful heart, which burns with love for the whole of creation – for humans, for birds, for the beasts, for demons – for all of God's creatures.'[5] And in the early part of the twentieth century, Fyodor Dostoevsky embraced the same truth in *The Brothers Karamazov*, relating – indeed, reconciling – compassion to forgiveness in the words of Staretz Zossima:

> Brothers, be not afraid of men's sins. Love man even in his sin, for that already bears the semblance of divine love and is the highest love on earth. Love all God's creation, the whole of it and every grain of sand. Love every leaf, every ray of God's light! Love the animals, love the plants, love everything. If you love everything, you will perceive the divine mystery in things. And once you have perceived it, you will begin to comprehend it ceaselessly more and more every day. And you will at last come to love the whole world with an abiding, universal love. Love the animals: God has given them the rudiments of thought and untroubled joy. Do not, therefore, trouble them, do not torture them, do not deprive them of their

joy, do not go against God's intent. Man, do not exalt yourself above the animals: they are without sin, while you
with your majesty defile the earth by your appearance on
it and you leave the traces of your defilement behind
you – alas, this is true of almost every one of us! Love children especially, for they, too, like the angels, are without
sin, and live to arouse tender feelings in us and to purify
our hearts, and are as a sort of guidance to us. Woe to him
who offends a child![6]

Father Zossima goes on to instruct young monks about the
need to struggle for forgiveness:

Brothers, love is a teacher, but one must know how to
acquire it, for it is acquired with difficulty, it is dearly
bought, one must spend a great deal of labour and time on
it, for we must love not only for a moment and fortu-
itously, but for ever. Anyone can love by accident, even the
wicked can do that. My young brother asked forgiveness
of the birds: it may seem absurd, but it is right nonetheless, for everything, like an ocean, flows and comes into
contact with everything else: touch it in one place and it
reverberates at the other end of the world. It may be mad-
ness to beg forgiveness of the birds, but, then, it would be
easier for the birds, and for the child, and for every animal
if you were yourself more pleasant than you are now –
just a little easier, anyhow. Everything is like an ocean, I
tell you. Then you would pray to the birds, too, consumed
by a universal love, as though in a sort of ecstasy, and
pray that they, too, should forgive your sin. Set great store
by this ecstasy, however absurd people may think it.[7]

Then, as a consequence to such embracing compassion,
Zossima concludes by relating compassionate love to cosmic
liturgy:

When you are left in solitude, pray. Love to fall upon the
earth and kiss it. Kiss the earth ceaselessly and love it
insatiably. Love all men, love everything, seek that

rapture and ecstasy. Water the earth with the tears of your joy and love those tears. Be not ashamed of that ecstasy, prize it, for it is a gift of God, a great gift, and it is not given to many, but only to the chosen ones.[8]

The world in its entirety forms an integral part of the liturgy. God is praised by the trees and by the birds, glorified by the stars and the moon (cf. Ps. 18:2), worshipped by the sea and the sand. There is a dimension of art, of music and of beauty in the world. This world is the most inconspicuous and silent sermon declaring the word of God. Indeed, for all intents and purposes, since most of us may not fully contemplate the spiritual depth of things, it is also the clearest, most visible and most tangible sermon declaring God's presence.

This means, however, that whenever we narrow life to ourselves – to our concerns and our desires – we neglect our vocation to reconcile and transform creation. And whenever we reduce our religious life to ourselves – to our concerns and our desires – we forget the function of the liturgy to implore God for the renewal of the whole polluted cosmos. Our relationship with this world determines our relationship with heaven. The way we treat the earth is reflected in the way that we pray to God.

Humanity, we now know, is *less than humanity* without the rest of creation. We may go further than this and declare that this world too is much more than a mere reflection or revelation of heaven; it is a fulfilment and completion of heaven. Heaven is *less than heaven* without this world. The earthly liturgy is not merely a con-celebration, but a completion of the heavenly dance. Just as we are incomplete without the rest of material and animal creation, so too the kingdom of God remains – daring and scandalous as it may seem – incomplete without the world around us. Not because of some inner or innate beauty and sacredness in the created world; but simply because that is how God chose to share the divine beauty and sacredness. How could we ever thank God enough for such a gift?

THE BODY OF THE WORLD

Of course, this world does not always feel or even look like some sort of completion of heaven. In his letter to the Colossians, St Paul writes: 'Through him [Christ], God was pleased to reconcile to himself all things, whether on earth or in heaven, by making peace through the blood of his cross' (1:20). Reference here to 'the blood of the cross' is a clear indication, at least for Orthodox spirituality, of the cost involved. It reminds us of the reality of human failure and of the need for a cosmic repentance. In order to alter our self-image, what is required is nothing less than a radical reversal of our perspectives and attitudes, especially of our practices and lifestyles. There is a price to pay for our wasting. It is the cost of self-discipline. The balance of the world has been ruptured; it is an 'outstanding balance' that can only be countered by the sacrifice of bearing the cross. The environmental crisis will not be solved simply by sentimental expressions of regret or aesthetic formulations of imagination. It is the 'tree of the cross' that reveals to us the way out of our ecological impasse by proposing the solution of – in theological terminology, this is called 'salvation' through – self-denial, the denial of selfishness or self-centredness. It is a spirit of asceticism that can lead to a spirit of gratitude and love, to the rediscovery of wonder and beauty in our relationship with the world.

The cross further raises the concept of asceticism or discipline of the heart and body as a way of relating to and reconciling with the world. For, the connection is intimate and profound between our body and our world. In the third century, Origen of Alexandria believed that 'The world is like our body. It too is formed of many limbs and directed by a single soul.'[9] If the earth is our very flesh, then it is also inseparable from our story, our destiny and our God. For 'no one ever hates one's own flesh' (Eph. 5:29).

The ascetic way is a way of liberation. And the ascetic is the person who is free, uncontrolled by attitudes that abuse the

world; uncompelled by ways that use the world; characterised
by self-control, by self-restraint and by the ability to say 'no' or
'enough'. Asceticism, then, aims at refinement, not detachment or destruction. Its goal is moderation, not repression. Its
content is positive, not negative: it looks to service, not
selfishness; to reconciliation, not renunciation or escape.
'Without asceticism, none of us is authentically human.'[10]

Let us examine one particular aspect of asceticism in the
Christian Orthodox spiritual practice, namely *fasting*. We
Orthodox fast from all dairy and meat products for half of the
entire year, almost as if in an effort to reconcile one half of the
year with the other, secular time with the time of the kingdom.
To fast is:

- not to deny the world, but to affirm the world, together
  with the body, as well as the material creation;
- to remember the hunger of others, identifying ourselves
  with – and not isolating ourselves from – the rest of the
  world;
- to feel the hunger of creation itself for restoration and
  transfiguration;
- to hunger for God, transforming the act of eating into
  nothing less than a sacrament;
- to remember that we live not 'by bread alone' (Matt. 4:4),
  that there is a spiritual dimension to our life;
- to feast along with the entire world; for if we Orthodox
  fast together – never alone or at whim – the ultimate
  purpose is to appreciate the natural beauty of all creation.

To fast is to acknowledge that all of this world, 'the earth, is the
Lord's, and all the fullness thereof' (Ps. 23:1). It is to affirm
that the material creation is not under our control; it is not to
be exploited selfishly, but is to be returned in thanks to God,
restored in communion with God.

Therefore, to fast is to learn to give, and not simply to give
up. It is not to deny, but in fact to offer, to learn to share, to
connect with the natural world. It is beginning to break down
barriers with my neighbour and my world, recognising in
others faces, icons; and in the earth, the face itself of God.

Anyone who does not love trees does not love people; anyone who does not love trees does not love God.

To fast, then, is to love; it is to see more clearly, to restore the primal vision of creation, the original beauty of the world. To fast is to move away from what I want, to what the world needs. It is to be liberated from greed, control and compulsion. It is to free creation itself from fear and destruction. Fasting is to value everything for itself, and not simply for ourselves. It is to regain a sense of wonder, to be filled with a sense of goodness, of God-liness. It is to see all things in God, and God in all things. The discipline of fasting is the necessary corrective for our culture of wasting. Letting go is the critical balance for our controlling; communion is the alternative for our consumption; and sharing is the only appropriate healing of the scarring that we have left on the body of our world, as well as on humanity as the body of God.

REGAINING A SENSE OF CONFESSION, COMMUNION AND COMPASSION

The Imperative of Confession

In order, however, to understand why we are losing ground in our environmental endeavours at the beginning of the twenty-first century, *we are called to remember and to confess* – as individuals and as institutions – where we have come, where we are and where we are headed. This critical process of self-assessment is vital. The sacrament of reconciliation or reconnection – in theological terminology, it is known as 'at-one-ment' – is still known by its classical name in the Orthodox Church, namely 'confession'.

The sacrament of confession is the process and privilege of recognising what we do and of reflecting on why we do it. It is assuming responsibility for our attitudes and actions, as well as for our inaction and perhaps indifference to action. Yet, the Greek word for 'confession' (*exomologesis*) implies more than this. It involves an opportunity to be thankful, and not so much to be remorseful. As human beings, fashioned in the image and likeness of God, we are endowed with the unique possibility to sin, as well as the unique blessing to choose the way we relate to people, animals and things. Our concern and our concerted efforts for the environment indicate in fact that we are, for the first time perhaps in history, able to direct our actions in a deliberately caring and compassionate way. It is up to us to shape our future; it is up to us to choose our destiny.

Far too long have we limited our understanding of sin to individual shortcomings and failures, at best appreciating their impact on other people. We have explored only the anthropological, or at best the sociological, implications of sin. It is time now to expand our notion of sin to encompass the effects of our actions on the natural environment. Speaking during a visit to the United States in 1997, Ecumenical Patriarch Bartholomew remarked:

> To commit a crime against the natural world is a sin. For humans to cause species to become extinct and to destroy the biological diversity of God's creation; for humans to degrade the integrity of the earth by causing changes in its climate, by stripping the earth of its natural forests, or destroying its wetlands; for humans to contaminate the earth's waters, its land, its air and its life with poisonous substances – these are sins.[11]

There is another dimension to confession and reconciliation, one that enables us to recognise our interconnectedness as human beings caring and struggling for the preservation of creation. The Greek term for 'confession' (*exomologesis*) further indicates a sense of similarity, even identity with one another. Indeed, we are more like one another in our weaknesses than in our strengths. We resemble one another more closely when we expose our shortcomings, rather than when we express our virtues. In openly admitting that we have done less than we could or should have for the preservation of our environment, we are in fact doing much more than we can ever imagine. To pretend, as concerned ecologists, that we are the environmental 'good Samaritans' is to ignore the reality that we are part of a community of environmental 'highway robbers'. I would be perpetuating the vicious cycle of human arrogance and dominance over the environment if I naively avoided owning up to my own failure and assuming my own responsibility.

The Imperative of Communion

And so, a sense of confession leads to the imperative of connection/communion. In a very distinctive way, the earth unites us all – before, and perhaps beyond, any and all doctrinal, political, racial or other differences. We may or may not share concepts and cultures. Yet we do share an experience of the environment; we share the air that we breathe, the water that we drink and the ground that we tread – albeit neither equally nor fairly. By some mysterious connection that we do not always understand and sometimes choose to ignore, the willingness to exploit and hurt people becomes a license to exploit and hurt the material creation. And, vice versa, the readiness to rape the natural environment opens the door to abusing human beings.

We are called to relearn the sense of communion or connectedness, that we are connected not only to one another, but also to the earth that binds us. And we will be judged, I believe, by the tenderness and delicacy with which we respond to nature – often a reflection of the way with which we treat human beings. Until and unless I am able to see in the face of the world the face of my own child, I will not be able to discern also in it the face of all faces, the face of my God. Then I can recognise in each tree and in each animal a face, and a name, and a time, and a place, and a voice that longs to be heard.

Far too often, however, we are sure that we have the solutions to the environmental crisis that we face, without being still to listen to the earth that we have so burdened and wounded. Let us not forget that it is our very actions that have led us in the first place to the situation we are facing. The present ecological crisis is not simply the result of bad judgement and vice, of greed and covetousness; it is also largely a result of human effort and success, of our struggle to develop a better world.

In his formative article entitled 'The Roots of our Ecological Crisis', Lynn White noted:

> The Greek saint contemplates; the Western saint acts. The Latins . . . felt that sin was moral evil, and that salvation was to be found in right conduct . . . The implications of Christianity for the conquest of nature would emerge more easily in the Western atmosphere.[12]

Ecological correction may in fact begin with environmental inaction. This is the discipline of silence, of vigilance and of detachment. It is the way of humility, of learning to tread lightly and gently. Humility connects us; pride divides us – from one another and from the earth. Indeed, pride is a uniquely human attribute; it belongs to Adam. There are, however, lessons of humility to be learned from indigenous peoples. In central Australia, for example, Aborigines of the Aranda tribe have totemic sites for the red kangaroo that coincide with the most popular habitats of this species. When Aboriginal people approach the kangaroo totemic sites, they do so in silence and reverence, with their eyes shut. Hunting is forbidden near these sites, and weapons have been laid down some way off. Thus the red kangaroos are protected near the best of their habitats.

Our role is to serve the sacred covenant between heaven and earth, a covenant that is a source of hope and a promise of new life. This testament is the most precious gift we have to offer our children.

The Imperative of Compassion

Nevertheless, the Greek term for 'forgiveness' (*synchoresis*) implies anything but a notion of moral obligation or legal concession. Rather, it includes a sense of openness or spaciousness; it signifies 'allowing room' for other people, other ways and other things. Regaining a sense of confession and connection leads to a third imperative, that of *remembering compassion*. We are called to extend the circle of compassion in order to reflect the abyss of divine compassion.

We are, I believe, called to regain a sense of compassion. For, whether we know it or not, indeed whether we like it or not, we participate in each other's having and in each other's not having. The fact that someone *has not* changes the character of my having: it undercuts my security and drives me to share. The fact that the earth itself is rapidly losing its natural resources obliges me to use less, want less, even need less. Just as we are not objects but subjects, so also are the non-rational animals. They too have feelings of joy and suffering. Even the natural environment experiences destruction and life. It, too, has a soul. It, too, enhances the beauty of life – both, I would dare to say, in this life *and* in the next. It is of course difficult to conceive of the great array of living organisms and micro-organisms in the same terms as I conceive Emily, my pet Pomeranian, because they have no centre for acting and feeling as one entity. Yet, whether their value is intrinsic or instrumental, they nonetheless surely also have a unique and distinct value.

God's relationship with humanity and nature is one of *infinite compassion*. In the theology of my own tradition, God shares his own self – the very energies of divine being – with the world so that the entire creation becomes a 'cosmic liturgy' and a 'burning bush of energy'. This direct engagement with human beings and the natural environment elicits an analogous response from the individual entities of creation. A note on a tuning fork can elicit a response from a piano because the piano already has in it a string tuned to the same note. So it is with God and the world. God acts in life by being received as compassion, a compassion that transforms. God is – and is within – the very constitution of our world. This is the distinctive teaching of panentheism, which neither classic theism nor pantheism are able to appreciate. If God were withdrawn from the world, the world would collapse.

THREE MODELS OF CARING FOR THE EARTH

Now, if our ecological prayer is gradually to begin moving from the distant periphery of an abstract theology to the centre stage of practical ministry, if Orthodox spirituality is to become 'incarnate', then there are three models or approaches that may be recommended. These three approaches are complementary.

The Biblical Model

According to this model, the Church must be in solidarity with the weakest part of creation. It must stand for the most vulnerable aspects of creation, the helpless or voiceless details of this world, which according to St Paul 'groan in travail, awaiting their liberation from the children of God' (Rom. 8:22). This implies a kind of cosmic 'liberation theology': 'One member of the body cannot say to another, "I have no need of you." On the contrary, those members of the body that seem to be weaker are indispensable . . . and our less respectable members are treated with great respect' (1 Cor. 12:20–25).

The earth is a member of our body, a part of our very flesh, inseparable from our story, our history and our destiny. In the same way as the God of Israel once heard the cry of the poor and the oppressed (Exod. 3 and John. 4), God also now hears the cry of the earth – of the dumb creatures and of silent nature. This is the biblical covenant, God's promise to the people of Israel: God listens to the world; God attends to the created world; God tends to the details of this earth.

The inherent weakness of this biblical model is that it is all too often neglected. We tend to forget, to be faithless to both heaven and earth. And so it must be complemented by a second model.

The Ascetic Model

Ascesis, as we have seen, is an appropriate corrective for the excess of our consumer society. We might imagine here the three 'Rs' of the ascetic life: renunciation, repentance and responsibility.

Renunciation is an ancient response – indeed, pre-Christian. It is also a universal response – even non-Christian (native, Aboriginal and Indian peoples know this very well). As we have seen, renunciation is a way of learning to share. It has social consequences; it reminds us to use material goods respectfully. Renunciation is about living simply and about simply living.

Repentance is a return to a God-given life 'according to nature'. In repentance, we confess that we do not share, that we are self-centred, that we in fact abuse the goods of the earth. Repentance is recognising that we have fallen short of our vocation 'to serve and preserve' (Gen. 2.15) the created environment.

Responsibility is the challenge; it is the choice that we all have before us. Having renounced whatever clutters our mind and our life, and after repenting of our wastefulness, we can direct our lives in a manner that is at once reverent towards creation and its Creator.

One qualification needs to be made here, which constitutes also the inherent weakness of the ascetic model. Ascesis is not another, a 'better' way of action, but in reality a way of inaction, of silence and of vigilance. We are called to remember that the present ecological crisis is a result of our action – of considerable human effort and impact – and not simply of human inaction and indifference.

The Sacramental Model

We have already seen how community is brought to bear in liturgy. It is here that all things are received and shared as gifts. The weakness of this particular model comes at the level of practice. For many of us, liturgy is confined to ritual observance; it is not seen as a way of active engagement. Yet, the broken body of Christ is not a way of pious or individual inspiration. It is an imperative for sharing. The sacraments, therefore, have an undeniable and indelible environmental seal.

Baptism. In a world where water is polluted and wasted, baptism highlights the connection between the Spirit of God and 'living water' that renews and sanctifies the face of the world.

Eucharist. This sacrament is pregnant with possibilities of deepening our awareness of communion. It challenges us to work for a just society, where food is shared and everyone has enough.

Confession. Reconciliation and forgiveness provide an opportunity – both for us as individuals and as communities – to focus on the wider implications of our actions on others and on the environment.

Ordination. This sacrament is a reminder that the priesthood is the royal vocation of all people. We are all invited to celebrate the presence of God in every corner of 'the cathedral of the universe'.

Chrismation. Our personal invitation to 'see Christ' and to recognise 'the seal of the gift of the Holy Spirit' in all places of his dominion: in the face of all people and on the face of the world.

Holy Unction. This is a way of pouring the 'oil of gladness' of God on the wounds or scars of the soul, of the body, of the earth, as well as a call to heal the brokenness of our heart and the shattered image of our environment.

Marriage. This celebration affirms the truth of the deeper unity between God and humanity, body and soul, matter and spirit, time and eternity, man and woman, heaven and earth.

Unfortunately, however, we have been alienated from the natural world; we have worshipped in a way that 'spiritualised' or 'de-materialised' nature and the sacraments. The natural world, indeed our very notion of sacrament, is not associated with the meaning of life. Yet liturgy is, literally speaking, vital. And in this way, the sacraments reconnect us to God and to the natural world, by drawing on its elements – water, bread, wine, oil, fire, light and darkness. The writers of the early Christian

Church believed that Christ's flesh was a sacrament (Ignatius of Antioch); they were convinced that our own flesh was a sacrament (Symeon the New Theologian); indeed, they claimed that the whole world was a sacrament (Maximus the Confessor).

8. SPIRITUAL DIRECTION: GUIDANCE THROUGH DARKNESS INTO LIGHT

We all have need of some Moses; someone very skilled, a healer. (John Climacus)

I gave up going to hear public sermons. I settled on another plan: by God's help, to look for an experienced and skilled person. (*The Way of a Pilgrim*)

The issue of forgiveness, along with the attendant matter of free will, is of central concern in the spiritual guidance of the human person. We all need someone from whom we can learn that we are loved and by whom we may be directed through the way of darkness. What is ultimately at stake here is our ability to experience freedom in communion with God, as opposed to pursuing a separated, autonomous, non-communal existence. This chapter explores the phenomenon of spiritual direction in the Eastern Orthodox spiritual tradition, especially as this is articulated in the classic spiritual guides themselves, namely the desert elders of Egypt, Palestine and Sinai.

Authority in the Orthodox Church is never supposed to be the monopoly of an ordained few (cf. Eph. 4:11–12), whether higher bishops or ordained clergy. While this is not always how things are in reality or in practice, authority is in fact the responsibility of all (cf. Eph. 5:34). Obedience is not supposed to be the obligation of an 'inferior' laity or lower clergy, but the requirement of all the faithful, both lay and ordained. Unfortunately, in the history of Christianity, centuries of institutionalism and clericalism, followed by the 'lay revolution', in conservative and anti-hierarchical churches alike, have rendered the concepts of authority and obedience problematic, indeed a point of contention and almost disdain.

Nevertheless, clergy and laity cannot exist without one another; spiritual elder and child must be existentially united. Together they constitute the living Body of Christ; together they experience the mystery of Christ. Any distinction between them is merely functional and provisional, not essential. What is essential is the relationship of love and trust in Christ. Unity lived out *even* in diversity is precisely the promise of God to his Church. Any form or expression of authority, then, must not be the expression of human pride but of humility before God, of assimilation to the divine hierarchy, and of obedience to the will of him who alone is called Father (cf. Matt. 23:9). Hierarchy exists in order to reveal the priestly vocation (cf. 1 Pet. 2:9) and function of all within a world that is beautifully ordered by its Creator as *cosmos*.

This communication with another person, the connection with a spiritual elder, is considered to have sacramental over-tones, reflecting the presence of Christ himself. Through this relationship with one's disciples, the spiritual elder is believed actually to be handing down Christ. In this association, the elder's loyalty to and love for the spiritual children become a creative way of tradition, a striking – even if inconspicuous – embodiment of spiritual authority. In the elder, the disciples encounter a paradigm of integrity and of authenticity, so long as the spiritual elder seeks to give nothing of himself or herself (cf. Gal. 2:20). 'I give only what God tells me to give,' said St Seraphim of Sarov, a popular *staretz* (or 'elder') of the Orthodox Church.[1]

If the language of this chapter offers the appearance of being exclusive to men, this reflects the reality of a practice that is often restricted to men. Nevertheless, it is helpful to remember at this point that men and women alike can offer spiritual direction. The sacrament of engendering disciples in the Spirit of God transcends distinctions of gender. In the desert of Egypt, as in the centuries that ensued, women offered spiritual direction and instruction. Indeed, spiritual direction opens the heart and the world to the realm of freedom, 'where there is no longer male or female' (Gal. 3:28).

Therefore, the figure of the spiritual elder illustrates the two fundamental levels on which the Church exists and functions in this world: the hierarchical and the spiritual, the outward and the inward, the institutional and the inspirational, ultimately the organisational and the charismatic. In this sense, the *geron* (Greek) or *staretz* (Russian) or *abba* (Coptic) exists alongside the Apostles. Although not necessarily ordained to be a presbyter through the episcopal laying-on of hands, the spiritual father or mother is nevertheless a prophetic person who has received his or her charisma from the Spirit of God. There is no formal act of appointment for the spiritual elder. Yet the disciples are ultimately able – confidently and confidentially – to point to the elder as a human being pregnant with God.

The above-mentioned dialectic or tension between establishment and charisma, between the priestly and prophetic function, has never really been officially resolved, but has in fact always characterised the life of the Eastern Church, at least since the age of Constantine. If not always harmonious and comfortable, this tension has nonetheless been a creative force. The monastic flight to the desert and the parish planted in the world are considered as being equally essential and complementary. Neither, of course, has been or is without its weaknesses: the world continues to be an unadmitted temptation and idol for those in the city; and monasticism tends to give rise to individualism and extremism. Nevertheless, together, there is a sense in which they preserve the integrity of the Gospel. Monasticism remains and provides a symbol of the kingdom, which is 'not of this world' (John 15:19); while the parish reminds the Church that Christ is present 'wherever two or three are gathered in his name' (Matt. 18:20).

Thus, Orthodox spiritual life often gives rise to charismatic leadership within its embrace. This charismatic atmosphere especially prevails in the desert, where personal obedience to a chosen elder precedes all formal power relations. The spiritual elder's authority is legitimate inasmuch as he or she is in turn subjected to and embodies the spiritual tradition of the Church in its entirety. When spiritual obedience responds to and tends towards communion, rather than to structures of worldly power, then it becomes a powerful ingredient in the building up of the body of the Church. In this regard, it has been noted:

> There is one thing more important than all possible books and ideas, and that is the example of an Orthodox *staretz*, before whom you can lay each of your thoughts and from whom you can hear not a more or less valuable private opinion, but the tested witness and judgment of an entire tradition.[2]

THE SPIRITUAL ELDER

The Russian Orthodox writer Fyodor Dostoevsky offers us this description of the elder, such as he had experienced in the person of Father Ambrose:

> What is such an elder? An elder is one who takes your soul, your will, into his soul and his will. When you choose an elder you renounce your own will and yield it to him in complete submission, complete self-negation. This novitiate, this terrible school of abnegation, is undertaken voluntarily, in the hope of self-conquest, of self-mastery, in order after a life of obedience, to attain to perfect freedom, that is from self; to escape the lot of those who have lived their whole life without finding their true selves in themselves.[3]

Such an elder merits the title *pneumatophoros* or 'Spirit-bearer', striving to be led as perfectly as possible through the immediate guidance of the Holy Spirit, rather than through individual powers or ambitions. This authority was promised by Christ himself who said: 'What you are to say will be given to you when the time comes, because it is not you who will be speaking, but the Spirit of your Father will speak in you' (Matt.

10:19–20). The genuine spiritual elder in turn becomes a spiritual leader, assisting in the rebirth and regeneration of others into the life of the Spirit. As a genuine ascetic and martyr, the elder gives '[his or her] blood and receives the Spirit'.[4]

Orthodox theology and spirituality, of course, knows only one Father 'who is in heaven' (Matt. 23:9), 'from whom every family, spiritual or natural takes its name' (Eph. 3:14). It likewise affirms the bond of sharing and solidarity, which develops through the spiritual begetting of others into the Body of Christ. Thus, in eleventh-century Byzantium, Nicetas Stethatos, the disciple of Symeon the New Theologian, is able to describe his relationship with his spiritual father as a life-giving bond:

> I am dead to the former world. How should I return backwards? I have a father according to the Spirit, from whom I receive each day the very pure milk of divine grace. I refer to my father in God. He is also my mother since he has begotten me in the Spirit, and he warms me in his embrace as a newly born baby.[5]

The spiritual elder gives birth to disciples through and in the Holy Spirit. The spiritual elder is, in this way, the servant of the Spirit – ever invoking and ever waiting upon the Holy Spirit. 'Without the Holy Spirit, shepherds and teachers would not exist in the Church,' claims St John Chrysostom.[6] The Holy Spirit legitimates the authority of the elder, or rather reveals the elder's authenticity as love. The Spirit is the 'giver of life', as the Orthodox Church prays daily; it offers life in all its forms: personal, interpersonal, communal, ecclesial, hierarchical. 'God is love' (1 John 4:16). This same Spirit is revealed as personal communion, in a person-to-person relationship. The Spirit of God makes possible true unity in diversity, and reconciles freedom and authority in the Church.

THE NOTION OF OBEDIENCE

In the Orthodox spiritual way, it is inimical to the life in Christ for anyone 'to act in isolation', as John Climacus says; it is always 'less damaging' to do things wearing the garb of obedience and service, allowing Christ to govern one's life 'without danger'.[7] Such a notion of obedience does not easily strike positive chords in our minds. So, how was it viewed in the ascetic literature of the past? Or rather, since the Eastern Church claims to be a privileged receptacle of that early ascetic tradition, how is it seen in Orthodox spirituality today? In a word, and echoing the content of previous chapters, obedience means carrying one's cross with joy, knowing that one is actually taking part in Christ's crucifixion – itself an act of the ultimate obedience. In the desert of Egypt, Abba Hyperechios would claim: 'Obedience is the best ornament of the monk. He who has acquired it will be heard by God, and he will stand beside the crucified with confidence, for the crucified Lord became obedient unto death (cf. Phil. 2:8)'.[8]

Where the crucifixion breaks down barriers between Creator and creation, disobedience forms a barrier between humanity and God (cf. Eph. 2:14). John Climacus characterises obedience as a form of inward 'martyrdom', while, in the sixth century, Abba Barsanuphius speaks of 'the shedding of blood'. It is a 'witness' (*martyria*) or 'confession' (*omologia*), which allows one actually to see God![9]

Obedience is, of course, an absolute response. One gives everything away and receives only in proportion to such giving. Moreover, obedience is sometimes said to be blind. We shall return to the peculiar notion of blind obedience below. In the spiritual tradition of the desert, even if the physician's prescription is wrong, taken in obedience it will heal![10] At times, obedience seems to reach the point of the absurd and irrational, although it is 'never illogical'.[11] The desert fathers stress blind obedience, even to behests that are ostensibly absurd; thus, Abba John the Dwarf is ordered to water a piece of dry wood. The command may even be apparently immoral: thus, Abba Saio is ordered to steal. By the same token, the Egyptian monastics stress fidelity and promptness in obedience: Abba Mark was copying the letter *omega* when his *geron* called him and he left the letter unfinished.[12] The pain experienced as a result of such obedience is likened by Climacus to an 'anaesthetic' given by the physician while the patient undergoes the cure, and so the burden of obedience ultimately becomes a way of reconciliation and comfort to the monk. In the final analysis, obedience can only be efficaciously broken when it comes to questions of faith.

The liberating effects of obedience, enhanced by related disciplines such as fasting and prayer, allow the spiritual disciple to 'breathe' God, while at the same time even mitigating the spiritual struggle against the vices. Ascetic authorities claim that those in obedience are attacked by only three of the eight classical vices, whereas hesychasts, namely those who live alone, must additionally face the challenge of the other five. It would seem that, for John Climacus, obedience constitutes a protective, preparatory stage, whereas *hesychia* marks the ideal, more advanced condition.[13] Still, obedience is understood to have a key role in undoing the destructive wilfulness of fallen human nature, leading to repentance and purification.

To repent is to redirect one's intellect, will and actions towards God. It marks a new condition, a transformation. Obedience means obedience unto death, and even beyond death. In the *Ladder*, the monk Akakios, in obedience to John the Sabbaite, overcomes even the fear and barrier of death through obedience! Obedience becomes a promise of resurrection. To be thus resurrected is to be transfigured in divine light: 'I have seen those who shone in obedience.'[14]

THE RELATIONSHIP WITH THE SPIRITUAL ELDER

The Orthodox Christian is called to liberation by way of the margins of self-renunciation, in the paradox of self-subjection to a spiritual elder. 'Those who seek to save their life will lose it, and those who lose their life will preserve it' (Luke 17:33); so Christ speaks in light of the day of his glorious Second Coming. The Christian lives in light of this day, in the wake of the age that is at hand and is yet to come. One gives oneself away in and for Christ; and one learns how to do this precisely through the relationship with an elder. 'Do you know someone who has fallen?' asked Abba Dorotheus in sixth-century Gaza. 'You can be certain that such a person has trusted himself.'[15]

This surrender of self is no easy task. As we have seen, the ascetic needs at times to go to extremes in cutting off the personal will and in acquiescing to the will of God. Yet the ascetic chooses to go to extremes because of the extremity of the fallen, self-enclosed condition. It is a liminal situation that requires equally unlimited measures.

Obedience to one's spiritual father is not like the submission that one is subjected to in the world; for, it ought to exist in the context of love. Without this special personal relationship, one gains nothing but a feeling of guilt from obedience. And such guilt defeats the purpose of obedience, which is spiritual liberation.

As in the case of one's bodily father or mother, the spiritual child loves and respects the spiritual father or mother. The relationship is not merely biological but deeply spiritual. Abba Barsanuphius, the Palestinian 'great *geron*' of the sixth century, observes that the spiritual father and child are 'of one soul'; they are in fact 'soul mates' in eternal love. Indeed, Barsanuphius goes further than this, claiming that the elder does more for us than we do! We shall return to this image below.

It bears reiteration that the spiritual elder does not aim at imposing rules and punishments, even in his or her admonitory role. Although also called 'a good manager', the elder is, for the disciple, above all 'an archetypal image', 'a rule', and 'a law'. Nevertheless, the elder never prescribes rules but rather becomes a personal rule or living model, not so much through his or her words as through example. 'Be their example, not their legislator' is the advice of Abba Poemen.[16]

THE SPIRITUAL ELDER AS SPONSOR

In a unique and refreshing passage, John Climacus further describes the spiritual leader as *anadochos*, the term used for a sponsor or godparent at the sacrament of baptism in the Orthodox Church. The concept signifies someone who assumes responsibility for another.[17] The source of this doctrine is Pauline: 'We who are strong ought to bear the failings of the weak' (Rom. 15:1). The spiritual elder does more than direct responsibly; the spiritual elder assumes direct responsibility for the disciple. Barsanuphius writes to a disciple: 'I assume and bear you, but on this condition: that you bear the keeping of my words and commandments.'[18] The spiritual elder does nothing less than to take on full responsibility for the souls of others, as the author of *The Ladder of Divine Ascent* would concur: 'There is an assuming of spiritual responsibility (*anadoche*) in the proper sense, which is a laying down of one's soul on behalf of the soul of one's neighbor *in every way*.'[19]

Such *anadoche* might be complete, as both Barsanuphius and John Climacus suggest, but it may also be partial. The spiritual elder may choose to undertake responsibility only for the sins of the past or perhaps for those of the immediate present. In *The Sayings of the Desert Fathers*, Abba Lot says: 'I will carry half of your fault with you.' Barsanuphius responds to one spiritual child: 'I care, then, for you more than you do; or rather, it is God who cares. However, should you want to cast *everything* on me on account of obedience, I accept this too.'[20] Thus the spiritual elder lifts burdens, bearing personal responsibility for these. This is strikingly illustrated by the following anecdote recounted in the *Ladder*:

> The old man read the note, smiled, lifted the brother, and said to him: 'My son, put your hand on my neck.' The brother did so. Then the great man said: 'Very well, brother. Now let this sin be on my neck for as many years as it has been or will be active within you. But from now on, you can ignore it.'[21]

This gesture may point to a ritual practice of penance in the early Church, preserved in the present custom of the priest laying his hand on the penitent's neck during confession. The act clearly implies a sense of love and solidarity with humankind; for the elder assumes the suffering of others, therefore 'bearing the cross' (Luke 14:24) of Christ himself. The spiritual elder should not, however, lift burdens that exceed one's own powers; for, the elder will have to account for all one's spiritual children at the Last Judgement (cf. Ezek. 3:20).[22]

Still, the spiritual guide would prefer his or her own damnation to that of the disciples. Although John Climacus himself does not develop this argument, it is certainly implicit in the *Ladder* and can be found explicitly both in the earlier and later classical patristic literature alike. The biblical source is Moses' petition to God on behalf of the people of Israel: 'Oh, how these people have committed a great sin, and have made for themselves a god of gold! Yet, now, if you will, forgive their sin; but if not, I pray, blot me out of your book, which you have written' (Exod. 32:31–32). In like manner, the Apostle Paul writes to the Church in Rome: 'I wish that I myself were accursed from Christ for my brethren' (Rom. 9:3). Echoing this sentiment, Barsanuphius prays to God: 'Master, either take me into your Kingdom with my children, or else wipe me also off your book.'[23] Such utterances especially highlight the power of the loving prayer of a righteous person, as the spiritual father or mother should be. Thus, indeed, the prayer of the elder 'avails much' (Jas. 5:16). In particular, however, these passages reflect the atoning love of the perfect one 'who knew no sin to be sin for us, that we might become the righteousness of God in this' (2 Cor. 5:21).

SPIRITUAL DIRECTION AS A WAY OF LOVE

In opening up to a spiritual elder, one allows the divine other into the whole of one's life. One cannot, however, achieve this alone. It is necessary to allow at least one other into the deepest recesses of the heart and mind, sharing every thought, emotion, insight, wound and joy with another person whom we trust completely. For most people, however, this is a difficult venture. It is not easy for most of us to open up to another person, revealing the vulnerable and darker aspects of our life.

We are today taught and encouraged from an early age to be strong and assertive, to handle matters alone. Yet, for the tradition of Orthodox spirituality, such a way is false. For we are members one of another, not islands unto ourselves.

People need others because often the wounds themselves are too deep to admit to oneself; sometimes, the evil is too painful to confront alone. The sign, according to the Orthodox spiritual way, that one is on the right track is the ability to share with someone else. This is, of course, precisely the essence of the sacrament of confession or reconciliation. To seek God may resemble an abstract search; to acquire purity of the soul may sometimes feel like an arbitrary goal; but to seek and find oneself in one's neighbour is to discover all four: God, purity, our selves and the other person. Perhaps this is what Antony of Egypt meant when he observed: 'Life and death is found in my neighbor.'[24] This is why, in confession, one discovers the abyss of sin and the mystery of grace alike.

Now, repentance should not be seen in terms of remorse, but rather in terms of reconciliation, restoration and reintegration. Confession is not some kind of transaction or deal; it defies mechanical definition and can never be reduced in a juridical manner merely to the – albeit significant – act of absolution. Confession is not any narcissistic self-reflection. As we have already noted, sin is always understood in Orthodox spirituality as a rupture in the 'I–Thou' relationship of the world; otherwise *metanoia* could easily lead to paranoia. Confession always issues in communion; it is ultimately the ability to utter, together with at least one person, 'our Father'. It is the Eucharist, the mystery of communion, lived out day by day.

During the Reformation, emphasis was increasingly laid on guilt and remission. Previously perhaps, the problem was obedient submissiveness to institutional authority. Today, although death, guilt and institutionalism are less obvious and threatening, yet they gnaw away in the form of frustration, stress and anxiety. This is the age when people die of depression, boredom and meaninglessness. We are always in the context of searching for meaning in life. In this respect, the practice of spiritual direction reveals that the ultimate content and reference point of meaning lies in the knowledge and vision of God in and through the other.

We all have a need to overcome the fear of death. The answer is, of course, found in the God of light and life, in the resurrected Christ. Everywhere that we see light and life, it is the same resurrected Christ that is experienced. So when a parent says to their child 'Everything is all right', they are actually making a metaphysical statement. When a lover says: 'I love you', they are saying that love is stronger than death (cf. Song of Songs). By the same analogy, when you confess to an elder, you are resurrecting Christ. Then, you can believe in God; because, then, you are no longer 'afraid, for he has overcome the world' (John 16:33) of death through love.

CONCLUDING REMARKS

In the absence of a spiritual elder, the Orthodox tradition encourages one to search for religious *communities* with an established life of prayer and silence. Moreover, a great deal of spiritual discipline and personal formation can be received from an ordered *daily rule* of prayer and liturgy, of balanced labour and recreation. This appears to have been the chief way in which many persons in the history of spirituality gained inner maturity. Finally, the powerful presence of spiritual elders in *prayer* and reflection – the invocation and meditation of those who have passed away but whose memory still guides and guards the community – can be evoked at all times and in all places by those who know how to trust and who wish to learn to love.

Of course, if a suitable elder cannot be readily found, then the ascetic tradition encourages one to turn to the *reading of Scripture* and the writings of the Church Fathers. The crucial point is always to look outside and beyond oneself, to open up oneself, to begin to trust another; for healing will come only once one learns to love, when one is willing to bear the burdens of others and assume responsibility for others.

Through this openness, one receives the power to transform the whole world, to the last speck of dust. Nothing is any longer trivial: everything is perceived, in the light of Mount Tabor, as uniquely contributing to one's spiritual formation and salvation. Then one no longer has expectations of a spiritual elder – imagining that person to be of a particular type – but only of oneself.

A spiritual elder is to be sought in prayer and repentance. Should one not find such an elder, then there still remains the call to prayer and repentance. For, if there is a certain iconic identification drawn between Christ and the spiritual elder, yet it is always Christ who remains the authentic image of the Father. It is to Christ ultimately that one is opened, laid bare for diagnosis and therapy. If you find a spiritual guide, writes Symeon the New Theologian, then tell that person your thoughts; if not, then simply raise your eyes prayerfully and humbly to Christ.[25] For the spiritual elder is ultimately called to reveal the living image of Christ, birthing us into the life in Christ.[26]

It is, in this respect, especially significant to recognise the inherent *flexibility* in the relationship between elder and disciple. Some spiritual leaders may be endowed with rare gifts of the Spirit, while others are simply able to provide only the very basic guidance that is required. Some disciples may need to contact their spiritual elder frequently, whereas others may be satisfied with and equally inspired by infrequent visits. One must never forget the dynamism of the unique moment of a personal encounter: Symeon the Elder held Christ only once in his arms; John the Forerunner met Christ once; and Mary of Egypt took communion but once in her life.

CONCLUSION: THE SCANDAL OF THE CROSS

Longing for death as for life. (Abba Isaac the Syrian)

I believe in the resurrection of the dead.
(Nicaean-Constantinopolitan Creed)

'Come, receive the light!'

With these words, an entire church, previously waiting in darkness, lights up in splendour. People's faces shine. It is Easter midnight. The night said to be brighter than any day. Everyone, young and old, whether born into or received into the Orthodox faith, knows by heart the chant that will be repeated over forty days, the song that colours the yearly cycle: 'Christ is risen from the dead.' In an age when we look for ways and moments to celebrate life, Easter marks the feast of feasts.

Yet the secret of this celebration, the mystery of the resurrection, lies deeper. It is found in the previous day of anticipation. It is already foreshadowed on the cross. Orthodox themselves sometimes forget the central significance of the cross, preferring to claim that they are a church of light and resurrection. Like most people, they too prefer to forego the stage of suffering, choosing to move directly to the final result. The two, however, are inextricably linked. The garden of the tomb is inseparable from the hill of Golgotha – so it is geographically in the city of Jerusalem, and so it is spiritually in the way of the heart.

Orthodox spirituality proclaims the profound truth behind the Pauline words: 'The one who has died is freed' (Rom. 6:7) and 'is transferred from death to life' (cf. 1 John 3:14). So the red of the Easter eggs is the colour of blood on the cross. Perhaps the reason we distinguish sharply between these two events is that we misunderstand the crucifixion in terms of extreme sacrifice, rather than in terms of ultimate love. The cross is a scandal of divine compassion, the climax in a series of unending manifestations of the defining characteristic of God towards the world, for the life of which he gave his only Son. It is the mystery of love and life. 'Behold,' as an Orthodox prayer reads, 'through the cross, joy has come to the whole world.'

On the cross, we encounter the struggle between *the power of love* (as it is revealed in Christ) and the *love of power* (as it is perceived by our world). The powerlessness of Christ has always threatened the powerfulness of the world. And the silence of the cross is the most eloquent sermon about the power of love. Despite what we know in ourselves and whatever we see in our world, the cross proclaims what love can and will achieve. The scandal of the cross is that, in spite of our wrongs and the wrongdoings of our world, God loves us to the point of death, even death on the cross.

The power of this world binds. This holds true in the social domination by one class over another, the economic submission of the poor to the rich, the authority of men over women in the workplace, the church or the house, the hurt of children by abusive parents, and the control of the soul by external fears or internal sins.

Yet, the powerlessness of Christ on the cross liberates.[1] Christ confronts power, and unmasks its coercion. He does battle with deeply rooted habits of aggression and competition. And his powerlessness robs violence of its force. On the cross, God's love reaches the extreme point of our desolation and desertion. No matter how far from God we may have travelled, we are never too far from him. We are never alone. Love has the final word, however unfair or cruel the situation. Love always transforms and heals.

On the cross, Christ meets sin with forgiveness and reconciliation. He counters domination with vulnerability. He overcomes hatred with love. He battles evil with goodness. He conquers darkness with light, and death with life.

It is very hard for us to grasp the word of the cross. It conceals the silence of God's vulnerability. Yet, if we have eyes to see and ears to hear, we shall discover it in many ways and places. In a child that is born when two people surrender defences, embrace in weakness, and love unconditionally. In the faces of people who forgive and are reconciled; wherever the barriers of bitterness and resentment are made to collapse by breaking the vicious cycle of hurt and alienation.

The cross is indeed the final word. In the paradox of the cross, problems and difficulties do not disappear. They simply appear in a new light. They are appreciated in a new perspective. We know differently. They are perceived in the light of the final age that is to come. We understand that, through them and beyond them all, there exists the invincible power of Christ's crucified love. The light of the cross is stronger than any darkness in the world.

The Greek word for Easter, *Pascha*, derives from the Hebrew meaning 'passover'. The crucifixion and the resurrection are a 'passing over' from survival to fullness of life, and from mere life to life in abundance. The tomb of Christ was not empty. It was open! It remains for us an open invitation.

The thunderous response to the Easter greeting is: 'Christ is truly Risen!'

NOTES

INTRODUCTION: LIGHT THROUGH DARKNESS

1. Cf. K. Ware, *The Orthodox Church* (Harmondsworth: Penguin, 1964); J. Meyendorff, *Christ in Eastern Christian Thought* (Washington DC: Corpus Books, 1969); J. Pelikan, *The Spirit of Eastern Christendom, 600–1700* (University of Chicago, 1974); and V. Lossky, *The Mystical Theology of the Eastern Church* (New York: St Vladimir's Seminary Press, 1976).
2. See C. Mango, *Byzantine Architecture* (New York: Rizzoli, 1985).
3. The title of an anthology of spiritual texts on prayer collected and edited in the eighteenth century by Nikodemus of Athos and Macarius of Corinth. Cf. G. Palmer, P. Sherrard and K. Ware (eds), *The Philokalia: The Complete Text*, 5 vols (London and Boston: Faber, 1979–2003).

1. ORTHODOX SPIRITUALITY: RECLAIMING THE VOCABULARY, REFOCUSING THE VISION

1. For an introduction to the fundamental features of Orthodox spirituality, see A Monk of the Eastern Church (Lev Gillet), *Orthodox Spirituality: An Outline of the Orthodox Ascetical and Mystical Tradition* (New York: St Vladimir's Seminary Press, 1996).
2. Cf. K. Norris, *Amazing Grace: A Vocabulary of Faith* (New York: Riverhead Books, 1998), p. 8.
3. Dumitru Staniloae described the contemporary tendency to identify spirituality with disengagement from the world as 'premature eschatologism'. See his *Ascetica si mistica orthodoxa* (Alba Iulia, 1993), p. 28 (in Romanian).
4. Poemen 137; in B. Ward (ed.), *The Sayings of the Desert Fathers* (Kalamazoo MI: Cistercian Publications, 1985).
5. In E. Wheeler (trans.), *Dorotheus of Gaza: Discourses and Sayings* (Kalamazoo MI: Cistercian Publications, 1977), pp. 138–9.
6. *Reflections* I, b and XV, d. Translation in J. Chryssavgis, *In the Heart of the Desert: The Spirituality of the Desert Fathers and Mothers* (Bloomington IN: World Wisdom Books, 2003).

7. Title of a seventh-century text by John Climacus; English translation in *The Classics of Western Spirituality* (New York: Paulist Press, 1982). This classic constitutes a central focus of the chapters that follow.
8. Doulas 1.
9. Agathon 11 and 12.
10. Poemen 29.
11. From a hymnographical phrase descriptive of the Virgin Mother of God in the Orthodox Church.

2. LITURGY AND SACRAMENT: THE WAY OF GRATITUDE AND GLORY

1. R. Taft, *Beyond East and West: Problems in Liturgical Understanding* (Washington DC: Pastoral Press, 1984), p. 116.
2. *Against Heresies* IV, 5.18 (*Patrologia Graeca* (hereafter *PG*) 6:1028).
3. *On the Holy Images* 11, 12 (*PG* 94:1297).
4. *On the Life in Christ*, Book IV, 1 (*PG* 150:584). English translation in the St Vladimir's Seminary Press edition (New York, 1974), p. 114.
5. *On the Holy Spirit*, ch. 27, in *Nicene and Post-Nicene Fathers*, vol. VIII (Grand Rapids MI: Eerdmans, 1952), p. 41 (my rendering).
6. See H. Wybrew, *The Orthodox Liturgy: The Development of the Eucharistic Liturgy in the Byzantine Rite* (New York: St Vladimir's Seminary Press, 1990).
7. See A. Schmemann, *Eucharist: Sacrament of the Kingdom* (New York: St Vladimir's Seminary Press, 1988).
8. *Mystagogical Catechesis*, pp. 5ff. and *On Faith and the Symbol* (*PG* 33:505–24).
9. Ed. R. Hugh Connolly (Oxford: The Clarendon Press, 1929), p. 120.
10. Cf. R. Taft, *The Great Entrance* (Rome: Orientalia Christiana Periodica, 1978), p. 35.
11. *On the First Epistle to the Corinthians* XXXVI (*PG* 61:313).
12. Gregory the Theologian, *Epistle I to Cleidonius* (*PG* 37:181).
13. *Homily I, i on Order in the Liturgy* (*PG* 56:97).
14. Cf. Origen of Alexandria in *PG* 13:1734. The notion of 'hearing' the Word underscores the significance of silence in liturgy. Orthodox Christians actually pray that they 'may be made worthy to hear the Holy Gospel'.
15. Cf. Ignatius of Antioch, *Letter to the Magnesians* VII.
16. Cf. Archimandrite Vasileios, *Hymn of Entry: Liturgy and Life in the Orthodox Church* (New York: St Vladimir's Seminary Press, 1984), pp. 76ff.
17. Cf. J. Zizioulas, *Being as Communion: Studies in Personhood and the Church* (New York: St Vladimir's Seminary Press, 1985); and A. Schmemann, *For the Life of the World: Sacraments and Orthodoxy* (New York: St Vladimir's Seminary Press, 1973).

3. THE WOUND OF KNOWLEDGE: THEOLOGY AS DARKNESS

1. Archimandrite Vasileios, *Hymn of Entry* (New York: St Vladimir's Seminary Press, 1984), pp. 131–2.
2. *Theological Oration* I, 3. Cf. *Nicene and Post-Nicene Fathers*, 2nd series, vol. VII (Grand Rapids MI: Eerdmans, 1952), p. 285 (my rendering).
3. S. Bulgakov, *The Orthodox Church* (London: Centenary Press, 1935), pp. 24, 37 and 45.
4. Symeon the New Theologian, *Catechetical Oration* XXXIX, 3–5, in *Classics of Western Spirituality* (New York: Paulist Press, 1980), pp. 311–13.
5. Isaac the Syrian, *Mystic Treatises VIII* (Greek text XXI), p. 71 (my rendering).
6. Cf. V. Lossky, *The Vision of God* (Leighton Buzzard UK: Faith Press, 1973). See also J. Meyendorff, *Byzantine Theology: Historical Trends and Doctrinal Themes* (New York: Fordham University Press, 1987).
7. *Orthodox Theology: An Introduction* (New York: St Vladimir's Seminary Press, 1978), pp. 98–9.
8. *The Ladder, To the Shepherd* 1 (*PG* 88:1165BC). See the Holy Transfiguration Monastery edition (Brookline, 1978), p. 231 (my rendering).
9. P. Sherrard, *The Greek East and the Latin West* (Euvoia, Greece: Denise Harvey Publications, 1992), pp. 51–2.
10. *On the Deity of the Son and the Spirit* (*PG* 46:557B).
11. *Life of Moses II*, 163 and 162. Cf. translation by A. Malherbe and E. Ferguson in *Classics of Western Spirituality* (New York: Paulist Press, 1978), pp. 94–5.
12. In *PG* 40:1275.
13. *On Mystical Theology* 5 (*PG* 3:1045D–1048B). For Gregory Palamas, cf. *Chapters* 78 (*PG* 150:1176).
14. *Letter* 234, 1 (*PG* 32:868–72).
15. Evagrius of Pontus, *Chapters on Prayer* 60 (*PG* 79:1180).
16. V. Lossky, *The Mystical Theology of the Eastern Church* (New York: St Vladimir's Seminary Press, 1976), pp. 42–3.
17. See his *Mystic Treatises* XIX (not in Greek text), 105.
18. Cf. Maximus the Confessor, *Chapters on Love* III, 99 (*PG* 90:1048).

4. TEARS AND BROKENNESS: THE WAY OF IMPERFECTION AND SPONTANEITY

1. The fullest treatment of the subject of tears is by I. Hausherr, *Penthos: The Doctrine of Compunction in the Christian East* (Kalamazoo MI: Cistercian Publications, 1982). See also K. Ware, Introduction to *The Ladder of John Climacus* in *Classics of Western Spirituality* (New York: Paulist Press, 1982), pp. 20–7.

2. Alonius 2. On the spirituality of the desert fathers and mothers, see John Chryssavgis, *In the Heart of the Desert* (Bloomington IN: World Wisdom Books, 2003).

3. Poemen 119 and Arsenius 41.

4. Poemen 119.

5. Poemen 144.

6. Cf. 5.1, in *PG* 88:728. References in this section are to the Step and paragraph in the *Ladder*, with the reference to the Migne series of *Patrologia Graeca* (vol. 88) in parentheses. Translations are my own. See John Chryssavgis, *John Climacus: From the Egyptian Desert to the Sinaite Mountain* (London: Ashgate, 2004).

7. See A. Schmemann, *Of Water and the Spirit: A Liturgical Study of Baptism* (New York: St Vladimir's Seminary Press, 1974).

8. For the 'Uninvited Guest', see 7.27 (*PG* 88:805D–808).

9. On the life and teaching of Symeon the New Theologian, see Archbishop B. Krivocheine, *In the Light of Christ* (New York: St Vladimir's Seminary Press, 1986); and H. Alfeev, *St. Symeon the New Theologian and Orthodox Tradition* (New York and Oxford: Oxford University Press, 2000).

10. *Catechesis* (hereafter *Cat.*) 22, 110–11. The *Catecheses* have appeared in a French critical edition by B. Krivocheine and J. Paramelle for *Sources Chrétiennes*, vol. 96 and translated into English by C. J. de Catanzaro for the *Classics of Western Spirituality*, vol. 21. Translations here are my own.

11. *Theological Chapters* 1, 101.

12. *Theological Chapters* 3, 12.

13. *Cat.* 4, 464–98.

14. *Hymn* 15, 250–61.

15. *Chapters of Thanksgiving* 2, 208–24.

16. *Cat.* 4, 203–5.

17. *Hymn* 50, 177–97.

18. *Ethical Discourses* 10, 873–88. See introduction and translation by A. Golitzin, *Symeon the New Theologian: On the Mystical Life. The Ethical Discourses*, 3 vols (New York: St Vladimir's Seminary Press, 1995).

19. *Cat.* 2, 211–12.

20. *Cat.* 23, 220–4.

21. *Theological Chapters* 3, 21.

5. A SILENT TRADITION: EARLY MONASTICISM AND CON-TEMPORARY EXPRESSIONS

1. Macarius 2.
2. Athanasius, *Life of Antony and The Letter to Marcellinus*, ch. 14 (London: SPCK; New York: Paulist Press, 1980), pp. 42–3.
3. For an account and analysis of these lifestyles, see D. Chitty, *The Desert a City: An Introduction to the Study of Egyptian and Palestinian Monasticism under the Christian Empire* (Oxford: Mowbray-Blackwell, 1966).
4. Climacus, *Step* 27.17 (*PG* 88:1100).
5. *Letter* 554. For a selection of the correspondence by Barsanuphius and John, see J. Chryssavgis, *Letters from the Desert* (New York: St Vladimir's Seminary Press, 2003).
6. Basil of Caesarea, *Epistle* 2, to Gregory (*PG* 32:224–33), vol. 8, in *Nicaean and Post-Nicaean Fathers* (Grand Rapids MI: Eerdmans, 1952), pp. 110–12.
7. On the Jesus Prayer, see I. Hausherr, *The Name of Jesus* (Kalamazoo: Cistercian Publications, 1978); and K. Ware, *The Power of the Name* (Oxford: Fairacres, 1974).
8. See J. Meyendorff, *St. Gregory Palamas and Orthodox Spirituality* (New York: St Vladimir's Seminary Press, 1974).
9. See K. Ware, Introduction to *The Art of Prayer* (London: Faber and Faber, 1966).
10. *Chapters on Prayer* 70, ed. J. E. Bamberger (Kalamazoo: Cistercian Publications, 1981), p. 66.
11. A. de Mendieta, *Mount Athos: The Garden of the Panaghia* (Berlin, 1972), p. 79.
12. See, for example, Gregory Nazianzen, *Second Theological Oration* 29.2 (*PG* 36:76); and Maximus the Confessor, *Question 60 to Thalassius* (*PG* 90:621).
13. Basil of Caesarea, *Epistle* 207 (*PG* 32:761). On Athonite prayer life, see P. Sherrard, *Athos: Mountain of Silence* (New York: Oxford University Press, 1960).
14. See Climacus, *Step* 27.10 (*PG* 88:1097).
15. Isaac of Syria, *Mystical Treatises*, ed. A. J. Wensinck (Amsterdam, 1923; Wiesbaden, 1965), p. 174.
16. Colleen McCullough, *The Thorn Birds* (New York: Avon Books, 1977), p. ix.
17. For an account of the numerous species on the forest-covered mountain, see P. Oswald, 'The Flora and Fauna of the Holy Mountain', *Friends of Mount Athos Annual Report 1995* (Oxford, 1996), pp. 35–9.
18. Palladius, *Lausiac History* 18 (Westminster MD: Newman Books, 1965), p. 67.
19. Climacus, *Step* 27.

6. PATHS OF CONTINUITY: CONTEMPORARY WITNESSES OF THE HESYCHAST EXPERIENCE

1. See Archimandrite Sophrony, *His Life Is Mine* (Oxford: Mowbray; New York: St Vladimir's Seminary Press, 1977), pp. 7–13. Cf. also N. Sakharov, *I Love, Therefore I Am: The Theological Legacy of Archimandrite Sophrony* (New York: St Vladimir's Seminary Press, 2002).
2. The book subsequently appeared in two separate parts with the titles *The Monk of Mount Athos* (the biography) and *Wisdom from Mount Athos* (the teachings), published by St Vladimir's Seminary Press, New York.
3. Archimandrite Sophrony, *His Life Is Mine*.
4. *ibid.*, p. 90.
5. *ibid.*, p. 112.
6. *ibid.*, p. 44.
7. *ibid.*, p. 89.
8. *ibid.*, p. 76.
9. *ibid.*, p. 85.
10. *ibid.*, p. 77.
11. *ibid.*, p. 44.
12. *ibid.*, p. 60.
13. *ibid.*, pp. 85–6.
14. *ibid.*, pp. 80–1.
15. *ibid.*, p. 73.
16. *ibid.*, p. 125.
17. *ibid.*, p. 87.
18. *ibid.*, pp. 108–9.
19. *ibid.*, p. 64.
20. *ibid.*, p. 59.
21. *ibid.*, pp. 61–2.
22. *ibid.*, pp. 74–5.
23. *ibid.*, p. 63.
24. *ibid.*, p. 68.
25. *ibid.*, p. 54.
26. *ibid.*, p. 110.
27. *ibid.*, p. 79.
28. *ibid.*, p. 81.
29. *ibid.*, p. 78.
30. Monk Joseph, *Elder Joseph the Hesychast: Struggles, Experiences, Teachings* (Mount Athos: Vatopedi Monastery, 1990), p. 30.
31. *ibid.*, p. 44.
32. *ibid.*, p. 125.
33. *ibid.*, p. 215.
34. *ibid.*, pp. 170–1.
35. *ibid.*, pp. 175–8.
36. *ibid.*, p. 203.

37. *ibid.*, p. 162.
38. *ibid.*, pp. 188–228.
39. *ibid.*, pp. 226–7.
40. *ibid.*, pp. 179–80.
41. *ibid.*, pp. 182–3.
42. *ibid.*, pp. 165 and 194.
43. *ibid.*, p. 195.
44. *ibid.*, pp. 197, 196 and 195.
45. *ibid.*, pp. 217 and 201.
46. *ibid.*, pp. 201 and 205.
47. *ibid.*, pp. 198–9.
48. *ibid.*, pp. 220 and 197.
49. *ibid.*, p. 228.
50. *ibid.*, pp. 207 and 217.
51. The Elder Paisios authored a very popular book on *Saint Arsenios of Cappadocia* (Thessaloniki: Convent of St John the Theologian, 1975), as well as two other books published by the same convent: *Elder Hatzi-Georgis the Athonite 1809–1886* (1986) and *Fathers and Stories of the Holy Mountain* (1993). The convent has recently published the elder's *Letters* (1994) and *Homilies*, vols. 1–3 (1998–2001).
52. For biographical and other anecdotal stories about the Elder Paisios, see Fr Christodoulos (Angeloglou), *Elder Paisios of the Holy Mountain* (Mount Athos, 1994 [English trans. 1998]); and *Chosen Vessel* (Mount Athos, 1996).
53. See, Christodoulos, *Elder Paisios*, p. 99.
54. Cf. Christodoulos, *Elder Paisios*, pp. 54–5.
55. *ibid.*, p. 59.
56. *ibid.*, p. 54.
57. *ibid.*, p. 53.
58. *ibid.*, p. 54.
59. *ibid.*, p. 138.
60. *ibid.*, pp. 26 and 29.
61. *ibid.*, p. 29.
62. *ibid.*, pp. 43–4.
63. *ibid.*, pp. 130–1 and 45.
64. *ibid.*, p. 36.
65. *ibid.*, p. 29.
66. *ibid.*, pp. 30 and 40.
67. *ibid.*, p. 30.
68. *ibid.*, pp. 45 and 58.
69. *ibid.*, p. 103.
70. *ibid.*, p. 145.
71. *ibid.*, pp. 33–4.
72. *ibid.*, pp. 112–13.
73. *ibid.*, pp. 63, 133 and 132.
74. *ibid.*, p. 119.

75. *ibid.*, pp. 130–1.
76. *ibid.*, p. 64.
77. *ibid.*, p. 86.
78. *ibid.*, p. 136.
79. *ibid.*, p. 135.

7. THE BOOK OF NATURE: THEOLOGY, ECOLOGY AND SPIRITUALITY

1. The Greek term 'heresy' (*airesis*) implies a partial or incomplete truth. Part of this chapter draws on my introduction to the ecological initiatives of Ecumenical Patriarch Bartholomew, entitled *Cosmic Grace, Humble Prayer* (Grand Rapids MI: Eerdmans Publications, 2003). See also P. Sherrard, *Human Image, World Image* (Ipswich UK: Golgonooza Press, 1990); K. Ware, *Through the Creation to the Creator* (London: Friends of the Center Papers, 1997); and John (Zizioulas) of Pergamon, 'Preserving God's Creation: Three Lectures on Theology and Ecology', *King's Theological Review* 12, 1989.
2. Abba Isaac the Syrian, *Ascetic Treatises* 65.
3. F. Dostoevsky, *The Brothers Karamazov*, quoted in N. Arseniev, *Mysticism and the Eastern Church* (Marburg: Student Christian Movement, 1926 [Reprint St Vladimir's Seminary Press (New York, 1979), pp. 118–19]).
4. On icons, see L. Ouspensky, *Theology of the Icon* (New York: St Vladimir's Seminary Press, 1992); and P. Evdokimov, *Art of the Icon: A Theology of Beauty* (Redondo Beach CA: Oakwood Publications, 1990).
5. *Mystic Treatises, Homily* 48 (Brookline: Holy Transfiguration Monastery, 1986), p. 30.
6. Dostoevsky, *The Brothers Karamozov* (Harmondsworth UK: Penguin, 1982), vol. 1, 375–6.
7. *ibid.*, p. 376.
8. *ibid.*, p. 379.
9. *On First Principles* II, I, 2–3 (*PG* 11:183).
10. Cf. K. Ware, 'The Way of the Ascetics: Negative or Affirmative' in V. Wimbush and R. Valantasis (eds), *Asceticism* (New York and Oxford: Oxford University Press, 1995), p. 13.
11. From an address delivered in Santa Barbara, California, November 1997. See *Cosmic Grace*, pp. 220–1.
12. *Science* 155 (March 1967):1203–7.

8. SPIRITUAL DIRECTION: GUIDANCE THROUGH DARK-NESS AND LIGHT

1. V. Zander, *St. Seraphim of Sarov* (London, 1975), p. 32.
2. Cf. K. Ware, 'The Spiritual Father in Orthodox Christianity' in *Cross Currents* (1974), 296. On the principles of spiritual direction, as well as the particular problems that arise from it, see also J. Allen, *Inner Way: Eastern Christian Spiritual Direction* (Grand Rapids MI: Eerdmans, 1993); and J. Chryssavgis, *Soul Mending: The Art of Spiritual Direction* (Brookline: Holy Cross Orthodox Press, 2000).
3. *The Brothers Karamazov*, trans. C. Garnett (New York: Modern Library, n.d.), p. 27.
4. *Sayings*, Longinus 5.
5. Cited in I. Hausherr, 'Vie de Symeon le Nouveau Theologien' in *Orientalia Christiana* (Rome, 1928), 61.
6. *PG* 50:463.
7. *Step* 8, 20 (*PG* 88:832; 28, 27 [1133] and 56 [1140]). See T. Colliander, *The Way of the Ascetics: The Ancient Tradition of Discipline and Inner Growth* (New York: St Vladimir's Seminary Press, 1985).
8. *Sayings*, Hyperechios 8.
9. *Step* 4, 10 (681); 15.6 (881) and 33 (888). The reference to Barsanuphius is from *Letter* 254.
10. *Step* 26, 21 (1021); 25, 49 (1000); and 24, 14 (984).
11. *Step* 4, 111 (720).
12. See *Sayings*, John the Dwarf 1 (*PG* 65:204).
13. *Step* 27, 11, 9 (1109).
14. *Step* 4, 111 (720–1).
15. *Teaching* 5, 6 (*PG* 88:1680).
16. *Sayings*, Poemen 174.
17. *Step* 4:104 (717B).
18. Barsanuphius, *Letter* 270.
19. *Letter to the Shepherd* 57 (1189AB).
20. Barsanuphius, *Letters* 39 and 169. For carrying half the weight, see Barsanuphius, *Letter* 168; for forgiveness of all sins since birth, cf. *Letters* 202 and 210.
21. *Step* 23:14 (980AB).
22. *Greek Life* 132.
23. Barsanuphius, *Letter* 110.
24. *Sayings*, Antony 9.
25. *Ethical Discourse* VII.399–405.
26. *Epistle* III.824–34.

CONCLUSION: THE SCANDAL OF THE CROSS

1. See D. Staniloae, *The Victory of the Cross* (Oxford: Fairacres Press, 1976).

SUGGESTED FURTHER READING

INTRODUCTION: LIGHT THROUGH DARKNESS

Giakalis, Ambrosios, *Images of the Divine: The Theology of Icons at the Seventh Ecumenical Council*. Leiden: E. J. Brill, 1994.

Limouris, Gennadios, *Icons: Windows on Eternity. Theology and Spirituality in Color*. Geneva: World Council of Churches, 1990.

Quenot, Michel, *The Icon: Window on the Kingdom*. New York: St Vladimir's Seminary Press, 1991.

Runciman, Steven, *Byzantine Style and Civilization*. New York: Penguin, 1990.

Runciman, Steven, *The Great Church in Captivity: A Study of the Patriarchate of Constantinople from the Eve of the Turkish Conquest to the Greek War of Independence*. Cambridge: Cambridge University Press, 1968.

Sherrard, Philip, *The Sacred in Life and Art*. Ipswich: Golgonooza Press, 1990.

Vaporis, Nomikos Michael, *Witnesses for Christ*. New York: St Vladimir's Seminary Press, 2000.

Walter, Christopher, *Art and Ritual of the Byzantine Church*. London: Variorum, 1982.

1. ORTHODOX SPIRITUALITY: RECLAIMING THE VOCABU- LARY, REFOCUSING THE VISION

Aumann, Jordan *et al.*, *Christian Spirituality East and West*. Chicago: Priority Press, 1968.

Bloom, Anthony, *Beginning to Pray*. New York: Paulist Press, 1970.

Bloom, Anthony, *Courage to Pray*. London: Darton, Longmann & Todd, 1974.

Clarke, Elizabeth, *Reading Renunciation: Asceticism and Scripture in Early Christianity*. Princeton: Princeton University Press, 1999.

McGinn, Bernard *et al., Christian Spirituality*. 3 vols. New York: Crossroad, 1985–89.

Mantzarides, Georgios, *Orthodox Spiritual Life*. Brookline MA: Holy Cross Orthodox Press, 1994.

Staniloae, Dumitru, *Theology and the Church*. New York: St Vladimir's Seminary Press, 1980.

Staniloae, Dumitru, *The Experience of God: Orthodox Dogmatic Theology*. 2 vols. Brookline MA: Holy Cross Orthodox Press, 1994 and 2000.

2. LITURGY AND SACRAMENT: THE WAY OF GRATITUDE AND GLORY

Breck, John, *The Power of the Word in the Worshiping Church*. New York: St Vladimir's Seminary Press, 1986.

Coniaris, Anthony, *Sacred Symbols that Speak*. Minneapolis MN: Light and Life Publications, 1985.

Gregorios, Mar Paulos, *The Joy of Freedom: Eastern Worship and Modern Man*. London: Lutterworth Press, 1967.

Schmemann, Alexander, *Liturgy and Tradition: Theological Reflections*. New York: St Vladimir's Seminary Press, 1990.

Taft, Robert, *The Liturgy of the Hours in East and West: The Origins of the Divine Office and Its Meaning for Today*. Collegeville MN: Liturgical Press, 1986.

Uspenskii, Nicholas, *Evening Worship in the Orthodox Church*. New York: St Vladimir's Seminary Press, 1985.

Ware, Kallistos, *Festal Menaion*. London: Faber, 1969.

Williams, Benjamin, *Orthodox Worship: A Living Continuity with the Temple, the Synagogue, and the Early Church*. Minneapolis MN: Light and Life Publications, 1990.

3. THE WOUND OF KNOWLEDGE: THEOLOGY AS DARKNESS

Florovsky, Georges, *Collected Works of Georges Florovsky*. 1st edn. Belmont MA: Nordland Publishing Co., 1972 (vols 4, 6–11 and 13–14 published by Buchervertriebsanstalt, Vaduz).

Lossky, Vladimir, *Mystical Theology of the Eastern Church*. London: J. Clarke, 1957; New York: St Vladimir's Seminary Press, 1976.

Lossky, Vladimir, *The Vision of God*. London: Faith Press, 1963.

Louth, Andrew, *Denys the Areopagite*. London: Geoffrey Chapman, 1989.

Mantzarides, Georgios, *The Deification of Man: St. Gregory Palamas and the Orthodox Tradition*. New York: St Vladimir's Seminary Press, 1984.

Meyendorff, John, *Byzantine Theology: Historical Trends and Doctrinal Themes*. New York: Fordham University Press, 1987.

Pelikan, Jaroslav, *The Christian Tradition: A History of the Development of Doctrine*, 5 vols. Chicago: Chicago University Press, 1971–89 (see especially, *The Spirit of Eastern Christendom (600–1700)*, vol. 2. Chicago: Chicago University Press, 1974).

Ugolnik, Anthony, *The Illuminating Icon*. Grand Rapids MI: Eerdmans, 1988.

4. TEARS AND BROKENNESS: THE WAY OF IMPERFECTION AND SPONTANEITY

Behr-Sigel, Elizabeth, *The Place of the Heart: An Introduction to Orthodox Spirituality*. Torrance CA: Oakwood Publications, 1992.

Bondi, Roberta, *To Pray and to Love: Conversations on Prayer with the Early Church*. Minneapolis MN: Fortress Press, 1991.

Evdokimov, Paul, *Ages of the Spiritual Life*. New York: St Vladimir's Seminary Press, 1998.

Krivocheine, Basil (Archbishop), *In the Light of Christ: Saint Symeon the New Theologian. Life, Spirituality, Doctrine*. New York: St Vladimir's Seminary Press, 1986.

Maloney, George, *Gold, Frankincense, and Myrrh: An Introduction to Eastern Christian Spirituality*. New York: Crossroad, 1997.

Maloney, George, *The Mystic of Fire and Light: St. Symeon the New Theologian*. Denville NJ: Dimension Books, 1975.

Stewart, Columba, *Cassian the Monk*. Oxford: Oxford University Press, 1998.

Ware, Kallistos, *The Inner Kingdom: Collected Works*, vol. 1. New York: St Vladimir's Seminary Press, 2000.

5. A SILENT TRADITION: EARLY MONASTICISM AND CONTEMPORARY EXPRESSIONS

Gillet, Lev (Monk of the Eastern Church), *The Jesus Prayer*. New York: St Vladimir's Seminary Press, 1987.

Gillet, Lev, *On the Invocation of the Name of Jesus*. San Bernardino CA: Borgo Press, 1986.

Gould, Graham, *The Desert Fathers on Monastic Community*. Oxford: Clarendon Press, 1993.

Kovalevsky, Pierre, *Saint Sergius and Russian Spirituality*. New York: St Vladimir's Seminary Press, 1976.

Meyendorff, John, *Byzantine Hesychasm: Historical, Theological, and Social Problems*. London: Variorum Reprints, 1974.

Meyendorff, John, *St. Gregory Palamas and Orthodox Spirituality*. New York: St Vladimir's Seminary Press, 1974.

Rousseau, Philip, *Pachomius: The Making of a Community in Fourth-Century Egypt*. Berkeley CA: University of California Press, 1985.

Sherrard, Philip, *Athos, the Holy Mountain*. Woodstock NY: Overlook Press, 1985.

6. PATHS OF CONTINUITY: CONTEMPORARY WITNESSES OF THE HESYCHAST EXPERIENCE

Alexander (ed.), *Father Arseny (1893–1973): Priest, Prisoner, Spiritual Father*. New York: St Vladimir's Seminary Press, 1998.
Cavarnos, Constantine, *Modern Orthodox Saints*. 1st edn. Belmont MA: Institute for Byzantine and Modern Greek Studies, 1971.
Hamant, Yves, *Alexander Men: Witness for Contemporary Russia (A Man for our Times)*. New York: St Vladimir's Seminary Press, 1995.
Matthew the Poor, *Communion of Love*. New York: St Vladimir's Seminary Press, 1984.
Plekon, Michael, *Living Icons: Persons of Faith in the Eastern Church*. Notre Dame IN: University of Notre Dame Press, 2002.
Sophrony, Archimandrite, *His Life Is Mine*. London: Mowbray, 1977.
Sophrony, Archimandrite, *We Shall See Him as He Is*. Essex: Monastery of St John the Baptist, 1988.
Vasileios, Archimandrite, *Ecology and Monasticism*. Montreal: Alexander Press, 1996.

7. THE BOOK OF NATURE: THEOLOGY, ECOLOGY AND SPIRITUALITY

Chryssavgis, John, *Beyond the Shattered Image: Orthodox Perspectives on the Environment*. Minneapolis MN: Light and Life Publications, 1999.
Gregorios, Mar Paulos, *The Human Presence: An Orthodox View of Nature*. Geneva: World Council of Churches, 1978.
Limouris, Gennadios, ed., *Justice, Peace, and the Integrity of Creation: Insights from Orthodoxy*. Geneva: World Council of Churches, 1990.
Meyendorff, John, *Christ in Eastern Christian Thought*. Washington DC: Corpus Books, 1969.
Nellas, Panayiotis, *Deification in Christ: Orthodox Perspectives on the Nature of the Human Person*. New York: St Vladimir's Seminary Press, 1987.
Sherrard, Philip, *The Eclipse of Man and Nature: An Enquiry into the Origins and Consequences of Modern Science*. West Stockbridge: Lindisfarne Press, 1989.
Thunberg, Lars, *Man and the Cosmos: The Vision of St. Maximus the Confessor*. New York: St Vladimir's Seminary Press, 1985.
Walker, Andrew and Costa Carras (eds), *Living Orthodoxy in the Modern World: Orthodox Christianity and Society*. New York: St Vladimir's Seminary Press, 2000.

8. SPIRITUAL DIRECTION: GUIDANCE THROUGH DARKNESS INTO LIGHT

The Way of a Pilgrim and *The Pilgrim Continues His Way*, trans. R. M. French. New York: HarperCollins, 1965.

Allen, Joseph, *Inner Way: Eastern Christian Spiritual Direction*. Grand Rapids MI: Eerdmans, 1993; Brookline MA: Holy Cross Orthodox Press, 2000.

Gregorios, Mar Paulos, *Freedom and Authority*. Madras: Christian Literature Society, 1974.

Hausherr, Irenee, *Spiritual Direction in the Early Christian East*. Kalamazoo MI: Cistercian Publications, 1990.

Jones, Alan, *Exploring Spiritual Direction*. San Francisco: Harper & Row, 1982.

Philippou, A. J. (ed.), *The Orthodox Ethos*. Oxford: Holywell Press, 1964.

Schmemann, Alexander, *Church, World, Mission: Reflections on Orthodoxy in the West*. New York: St Vladimir's Seminary Press, 1979.

Turner, H. J. M., *St. Symeon the New Theologian and Spiritual Fatherhood*. New York: E. J. Brill, 1990.

CONCLUSION: THE SCANDAL OF THE CROSS

Arseniev, Nicholas, *Mysticism and the Eastern Church*. New York: St Vladimir's Seminary Press, 1979.

Bulgakov, Sergei, *The Orthodox Church*. New York: St Vladimir's Seminary Press, 1988.

Clément, Olivier, *Conversations with Ecumenical Patriarch Bartholomew I*. New York: St Vladimir's Seminary Press, 1997.

Louth, Andrew, *Discerning the Mystery*. Oxford: Oxford University Press, 1983.

Paul, Archbishop of Finland, *The Faith We Hold*. New York: St Vladimir's Seminary Press, 1980.

Ware, Kallistos, *The Orthodox Church*. 2nd edn. London: Penguin Books, 1993.

Ware, Kallistos, *The Orthodox Way*. New York: St Vladimir's Seminary Press, 1995.

Yannaras, Christos, *Elements of Faith: An Introduction to Orthodox Theology*. Edinburgh: T & T Clark, 1991.